DEMONS &
DEMIGODS

APARNA JHA

DEMONS & DEMIGODS

Death Penalty in India

OXFORD
UNIVERSITY PRESS

OXFORD
UNIVERSITY PRESS

Oxford University Press is a department of the University of Oxford.
It furthers the University's objective of excellence in research, scholarship,
and education by publishing worldwide. Oxford is a registered trademark of
Oxford University Press in the UK and in certain other countries.

Published in India by
Oxford University Press
2/11 Ground Floor, Ansari Road, Daryaganj, New Delhi 110 002, India

ISBN-13 (print edition): 978-0-19-948963-3
ISBN-10 (print edition): 0-19-948963-7

ISBN-13 (eBook): 978-0-19-909546-9
ISBN-10 (eBook): 0-19-909546-9

Typeset in Trump Mediaeval LT Std 9.5/14.5
by The Graphics Solution, New Delhi 110 092
Printed in India by Replika Press Pvt. Ltd

To my parents

Contents

ACKNOWLEDGEMENTS

I'd like to thank the following people: My agent, Divya Dubey, who helped me write. 'I refuse to touch your manuscript till you learn the craft [of writing] by reading these books!' Her persistence helped in polishing the work. My husband, Braj, and my kids, Mythili and Siddid, for leaving me alone to work in peace. Justice Patnaik and Nisha Saxena from Supreme Court Legal Services Committee, whose encouragement helped a lot in finishing the book. And, of course, the team at Oxford University Press India for their patience.

I

THE CASE OF THE FOUR BOYS

———

I am a lawyer. I practise in the Supreme Court. The courtrooms with high ceilings and wooden panels have become my second home. I joined the profession in 1995 and, soon after, began working at the Delhi branch office of Gagrat & Company, a solicitors firm based in Mumbai. I remember sitting and working in my senior's office. There were cubicles in a row where the lawyers sat and worked on their briefs. Our office was in Connaught Place, in the same building as Plaza Cinema. It was interesting to see puzzled looks on the faces of moviegoers as we moved up and down the stairs with paper and pen in hand. But we liked it best when our senior went to Mumbai, which he often did, for then we would sneak into the cinema hall and watch a movie for about an hour or so before it was time to leave.

Eventually, I ended up at the Supreme Court. The top court, with its magnificent building, a legacy of the colonial rulers, was the place I spent most of my waking hours, reading, revising, arguing. The corridors of the court are long and endless, and walking from one end to the other, to different courtrooms, can be tiring. Occasionally I would doze off in court, waiting for my turn. Waking up with a start, I would glance at the judges. Had they caught me napping?

And then one day a case was offered to me through a letter, dated 23 December 2011, by the Secretary, Supreme Court Legal Aid Services. I was asked to defend a boy on death row, Karim.[1] Would I be interested in taking on a death penalty case?

There were four accused—Ramesh, Salim, Karim, and Shyam—all young boys in their twenties. Ramesh's case was also offered to me through a letter dated 17 July 2012. All four boys came from Mumbai, Maharashtra, and were from poor families. While Ramesh drove a taxi in Mumbai, Karim ran a ration shop. Salim was an LIC agent, and Shyam worked for a private institution. I was to fight for Ramesh and Karim, while Salim and Shyam were represented by Shivaji M. Jadhav, an advocate on record in the Supreme Court who is presently the president of the Supreme Court Advocates on Record Association.

The Supreme Court Legal Aid Services is a body that provides free legal aid to the poorer and weaker sections of society. While I was to draft the matter and file it in the capacity of an advocate on record, P.S. Narsimha, also on the panel of Legal Aid, and presently the additional solicitor general of India, was appointed as the senior lawyer who would argue the case for the two boys.

In the Supreme Court, there are two categories of lawyers—advocates on record and senior advocates. Advocates on record have to pass an examination, the pass percentage being only 17 to 18. This is done for quality control, as the Supreme Court is the last hope for those convicted, with no scope for further appeal. Seniors are designated by the judges based on their knowledge of the law. I, as an advocate on record, was required to draft the case after I had researched the death penalty law and studied the papers sent to me, neatly typed in single space.

However, when the matter was finally argued, I represented all four boys. Colin Gonsalves, a senior lawyer of repute practising in the Supreme Court, known globally for contributing substantially to the field of human rights, formed a team with me to defend them.

The clerk came with the letter of assignment. Written on top in bold letters was 'Most Urgent, Out Today'. Death sentence matters are given top priority in the Supreme Court. When someone's life is being taken away by the state, their case needs to be heard without delay.

It was alleged that my clients were serial killers and had hacked 10 able-bodied people to death. They would carry bags full of arms—swords, rods, muzzle-loader guns—and would then take their victims, mostly gullible businessmen, to a hillock and kill them. The bodies were then chopped and strewn around. The body parts were discovered later by the cops: a half-eaten hand, a headless torso of a woman crawling with maggots. At times, these bodies were put in gunny bags.

No matter what, I could not let these boys hang. I began preparing for the case. In the following days, every scrap of paper that came to me was stamped with the heading, 'Most Urgent, Out Today'.

I do not believe in the death penalty. I do not believe anyone—absolutely anyone—has the right to take away a human's life. Maybe my clients had committed a heinous crime—nobody could deny this *if* they were guilty—but I could not let them die. I had to do everything in my power to stop the court from hanging them.

As in the West, the death penalty jurisprudence has been widely debated in India. I began my research on the case finder Supreme Court Cases Online, which has a database of cases and law. My clerk would note down the citations, and a little later, thick volumes on existing cases, with the words 'Supreme Court Cases' and the year of publication embossed in gold, would be stacked on my table. I had to go through those judgments before I began preparing my own arguments. Unless I understood the death penalty law in India, I could not proceed further. I had little experience in this area, and yet four lives now depended on me and my senior colleague. I knew that if I let them down, there would be nobody else to help them. Unlike me, my peers believed the boys had got what they deserved, that they were responsible for their own fate. I felt otherwise. They were little more than children. How could I simply let them be killed—even by the state?

Images of the boys hanging with a thick noose around their necks, their bodies dangling loose, flashed through my mind. I had never met them; they were in jail, in isolation, but I could imagine their terrified faces. I could see them huddled in a corner, waiting for the final verdict. They were not very educated—I had found that out from the papers. While one had studied up to the tenth grade, the other was even less qualified.

Had they really done it?

And supposing they had, why hang them? Even if they were serial killers, why *hang*? It reminded me of primitive times when the justice givers would chop off the hands and legs of the criminals.

I rose and drank a glass of water. After a while, I sat down and studied some more cases. I noticed that in some judgments that had been delivered by the top court, the death penalty had been commuted to life imprisonment. I wondered what they would do to my boys. The case against them had been watertight in the lower courts. I was responsible for whatever happened to them now.

What had been the courts' stand in cases similar to mine? I scanned the judgments relevant to my case from 1950 onwards, when the Indian Supreme Court was set up. Oh, it was a Herculean task searching for judgments and plodding through each! I read them one after the other, making notes. Some of them were quite long. I flagged the relevant pages, downing innumerable cups of tea.

For decades, I noticed, the top court had debated on the death penalty. If the victim had been roasted alive, the culprit was to be hanged. The state would show no mercy to those who had revelled in burning men and women alive, deaf to their pleas for mercy. The guilty could, however, be spared if they had been in jail for a long time, or if they were old and frail by the time their case reached the top court. They had already died a thousand times by then, and it was thought that hanging would really serve no purpose.

If a murdered person's body had been chopped off or destroyed in a fiendish manner, or if the accused was a serial killer, showing no remorse or mercy, they deserved no sympathy from the state.

I could understand now why both the lower courts had awarded death to the boys. Indian law is based on the British Common Law. Thus, the Indian judicial system is pyramidal in structure, and all guidelines laid down by the top court are studied minutely and followed by the lower courts.

My next step was to study in detail all those judgments and guidelines before I started working on my own case in full swing.

Note

1. The names of the four accused have been changed.

2

JAGMOHAN SINGH

———

I noticed there were two constitution bench judgments (decisions rendered by five judges) by the top court on the issue of the death penalty. The question before them: Was the death penalty unconstitutional? Did it take away the fundamental rights of a human being guaranteed by the Constitution—the holy book guiding the lawmakers and interpreters of the law?

In Case I, a man called Jagmohan Singh from Shahjahanpur, Uttar Pradesh (UP), was convicted under Section (S.) 302 of the IPC for the murder of one Chhotey Singh. The latter was murdered on 10 September 1969. It was a classic case of revenge and retribution.

Six or seven years earlier, Jagmohan's uncle, Shivraj Singh, had been murdered by Chhotey Singh, his relative, who lived next door to him in Shahjahanpur. The men had farms adjacent to each other. Chhotey Singh had been let off by the UP High Court. The victim, Shivraj Singh, had a son called Jagbir, who was around Jagmohan's age and was an accessory in the murder of Chhotey Singh. When Shivraj was murdered, both the cousins—Jagmohan and Jagbir—were minors. But the boys harboured a deep hatred for Shivraj's murderer, which only grew with age.

Chhotey Singh was murdered at about 5 p.m.—when the sun was about to set and the sky was a soft orange. The sun might have lost its ferocity, but Jagmohan and his cousin had not. Incidentally, the parties had fought a day earlier over the irrigation of their fields and the dispute had been settled by some villagers who had reached the spot on time.

Jagmohan carried a country-made pistol, while Jagbir Singh wielded a lathi. They hid in the bajra fields. They had decided to strike when Chhotey Singh crossed the fields on his way to buy fodder, as he did every week. Jagmohan fired a single shot. The bullet hit the victim in his back. He fell down and died.

The sessions court in Shahjahanpur decided that the culprits should be hanged. The high court upheld the extreme punishment and observed that there were no extenuating circumstances; the sentence of death was just and proper. A Special Leave Petition was filed in the Supreme Court, limited to the question of sentence: to hang or not to hang?

The judges of the top court pondered over the issue. They noted that even in countries like the US, laws relating to death were enforced in a discriminatory manner. Usually, the poor, the despised, and the unpopular minority—that is, the African Americans—were at the receiving end. But they said that capital punishment was not unusual, as this kind of punishment had been followed since ancient times. Our statutes provided procedural safeguards.

An accused charged with murder had to appear before the magistrate who, upon the examination of evidence, committed him to the sessions court for trial. At this stage, he or she knew the evidence against him or her. The trial took place before the sessions judge or the additional sessions judge, who had considerable experience in conducting trials. There was a provision of an appeal (for the accused) before the high court and finally the Supreme Court.

Earlier, when a person was convicted for murder under S. 302 of the Indian Penal Code (IPC), the punishment was either death or imprisonment for life. Section 367 (5) of the Criminal Procedure Code (CrPC) provided that the normal punishment for murder was death, while a lesser punishment of life imprisonment was given only after receiving special reasons in writing. The norm was to hang the convict, except in some exceptional cases.

But when Jagmohan's case came up before the top court, S. 367 (5) of the CrPC had been deleted by an amendment in 1955. It was left to the courts to decide whether to hang him or give him life sentence.

Jagmohan's lawyer argued that the awful duty of deciding whether to hang or to give life sentence was up to the judges. The view could be highly subjective in the absence of official guidelines—factors that would help the judges in choosing the right punishment.

The top court refused to accept this plea. The procedural safeguards provided in the CrPC and the provision of appeal protected the accused sufficiently.

It was difficult to lay down standards to determine the circumstances in which a person should be hanged or spared, said the court. It was simply impossible. Consider this: S. 326 of the IPC provided punishment for inflicting grievous injury by a dangerous weapon or other means. Suppose someone attacked a person with a dangerous weapon, resulting in a slight fracture of an unimportant bone, and another attacker scooped out the victim's eye with a spoon. It would be absurd to say that both the culprits should be given the same punishment.

Jagmohan's case was decided by five judges on 3 October 1972, with Justice Palekar writing on behalf of the bench.[1] The CrPC was amended, yet again, after the judgment in this case. Section 354 (3) was inserted. It stated that when a man was convicted for murder, special reasons should be given for imposing a sentence of death. This was a shift from the earlier stand, when death penalty was the norm and giving life imprisonment an exception. Laws were slowly being made less cruel.

I now decided to read the next constitution bench judgment of the top court, which again decided that the death penalty was constitutional, albeit with some changes. I picked up the next volume, which was kept on the edge of my study table.

Note

1. Jagmohan Singh vs State of U.P. (1973) 1 SCC 20

3

BACHAN SINGH

A discussion on the death penalty laws in India would be incomplete without the mention of the law laid down by the top court in the case of Bachan Singh—convicted for the murder of his wife, and sentenced to life imprisonment.

After serving his sentence, he went to live with his cousin, Hukam Singh, in Ferozepur, Punjab, for about six months. But Hukam Singh's wife and his son, Desa Singh, objected to this. They did not want a man who had killed his wife staying with them. They urged Hukam Singh to make Bachan Singh leave at the earliest. Bachan Singh was furious. The killer in him woke up and wanted revenge.

Some time later, Hukam Singh and his wife left for Nainital to fix Desa Singh's marriage. They had left Desa Singh at home with their three daughters. Bachan Singh hatched a plan. On 4 July 1977, he rose in the middle of the night while Hukam Singh's daughters lay asleep in the inner courtyard. Durga Bai slept on one cot, Vidya Bai and Veeran Bai slept on another.

Vidya Bai woke up with a start to see Bachan Singh standing before her with an axe in hand. He struck Veeran Bai on her face. Veeran Bai gripped her cot for support, struggling to rise, while Bachan Singh turned to Vidya Bai. The blow to her face came with such force that it injured her ear; she fell down unconscious. Dewan Singh, a relative who was sleeping nearby, saw Bachan Singh attack Durga Bai next. Gulab Singh, another relative who lay asleep about 50 feet away from Desa Singh, woke up and saw Bachan Singh strike the boy on his neck.

His anger spent, Bachan Singh flung his axe and ran away. Gulab Singh and Dewan Singh chased him, but could not catch Bachan Singh. The two men took the injured in a tractor to a hospital in Fazilka. Except for Vidya Bai, all the others died in hospital.

Bachan Singh was tried for killing Desa Singh, Durga Bai, and Veeran Bai, and for seriously injuring Vidya Bai. The latter became an important eyewitness in the case.

The trial court and the high court wanted to hang Bachan Singh. The case reached the top court. On 4 May 1979, two judges decided to refer it to a larger bench.[1]

The case was then referred to five judges, who debated on whether the death penalty was constitutional. It was a long judgment, taking note of the arguments of those who wanted the death penalty to be abolished, as well as those who felt it should be retained. The counsel for Bachan Singh argued that retention of the death penalty was not based on reason and purpose. It took away the basic constitutional rights of the person on death row.

The court, however, noted that people the world over—including sociologists, legislators, jurists, judges, and administrators—still believed that capital punishment protected society. It was ultimately held by the five judges that the death penalty was constitutional. Death could be awarded in the 'rarest of the rare' cases. The death sentence, however, was not to be a rule but an exception.[2]

Capital punishment was now to be given in the rarest of rare cases, and a set of aggravating and mitigating circumstances were drawn up while choosing the sentence. For citing special reasons in favour of the choice of the punishment, the court had to consider the crime as well as the criminal. The aggravating or mitigating factors depended on different facts and circumstances in each case.

'In a sense, to kill is to be cruel, and therefore all murders are cruel,' the top court had observed in its judgment in Bachan Singh's case, while reiterating that cruelty may differ in degree, and it is only when the murder is extremely depraved that special reasons should be given.

It was also observed in the judgment that 'the judges should not be bloodthirsty, for hanging of murderers has never been too good for them'. The concern for human life encouraged sparing a life when and where possible. Of the five judges who had heard this case, four were of the view that the death penalty was constitutional.

The fifth judge, Justice Bhagwati, disagreed, and expressed his views on the death penalty in a separate judgment. He felt that S. 302 of the IPC, which provided for death sentence, violated Articles 14 and 21 of the Constitution. These laid down that every person was equal before the law and had a right to life and personal liberty. He struck down S. 302 as being unconstitutional.

The grim reality is that the trial courts in India are giving a go-by to 'the rarest of the rare doctrine', and the number of death sentences awarded by these courts is very high.

Though the top court refused to restrict judicial discretion by making an exhaustive list of aggravating and mitigating factors, some guidelines *were* laid down. A balance sheet had to be drawn after both kinds of circumstances had been considered in a case. The mitigating circumstances included offence committed under the influence of extreme mental or emotional disturbance, or the age of the accused (that is, if the attacker was very young or very old). A young mind was immature, unable to differentiate between right and wrong. Therefore, they decided that the young should not be hanged if they had done something in a fit of passion. Likewise, the court felt that an old and frail convict would hardly be a threat to the society. They should not face the hangman's noose.

Post-murder remorse was, again, considered a mitigating factor. It implied that the accused could be reformed. In that case, they were to be pardoned. The fact that the accused had acted under duress or domination of another person, or that they thought they had been morally justified in killing their victims was also a mitigating factor.

I knew it was alleged that my boys had killed 10 people in a most horrific manner. How would the top court view the act? But they were young boys, too. I noted this down and went through the papers to find out exactly how old they were when they had supposedly killed.

The top court discussed all the aspects of death penalty at length. Another point to be considered while deciding whether a person should be hanged or spared was their mental state. A mentally unstable person did not know what they were doing. They were like children, unaware of the consequences of their actions. The judges felt that such a person did not deserve to die.

The court also gave some examples of aggravating circumstances where the death penalty should be given. For example, when the offender had killed someone who belonged to a Scheduled Caste or a Scheduled Tribe, that is, in brutal killings of those who belonged to the backward castes.

Another aggravating circumstance was the killing of a national leader, a policeman, or a public servant on duty. If the murder involved extreme depravity or brutality, or was planned, it was yet another aggravating factor.

Bachan Singh became a landmark judgment delivered by the Supreme Court. From then on, every case of murder was judged with Bachan Singh's case as the yardstick before a decision was finally taken.

In every murder case I have handled—and there have been many—I have seen that after an order of conviction is passed, that is, when the court holds that the victim is guilty of murder, arguments are led on sentence as the next step. Invariably, the public prosecutor argues in a mechanical manner that the case belongs to the 'rarest of the rare' category, and that death, the maximum punishment, should be awarded to the criminal.

There have been cases in which the victim was raped and killed, or stabbed or struck with a weapon in their vital organs, leading to instant death. And in every such case the trial judge would record the arguments of the public prosecutor as, 'Learned public prosecutor submits that the case is brutal, falling in the category of the "rarest of rare", and the accused deserves the death penalty.'

Agreed, in some cases the killing really is brutal and would shock the conscience of society. However, a single gunshot injury or a blow on the head with a stick, even though it may lead to instant death, cannot be seen as a 'rarest of the rare' case.

Would the Supreme Court confirm the death penalty in my case? The facts were awful, I knew, and it would be very difficult for me to convince the judges that my boys should be spared. I had not met their mothers, not before it was time for final arguments in the Supreme Court, but I could imagine what they were going through. It pained me. I rose to pick up the next volume from my book shelf where even more books on the subject stood in a row.

Notes

1. Bachan Singh vs State of Punjab (1979) 3 SCC 727
2. Bachan Singh vs State of Punjab (1980) 2 SCC 684

4

MACHHI SINGH

———

One of the most horrific cases I studied was that of Machhi Singh.[1] It was about a feud between two families, though the exact cause of the vendetta is not known. It is amazing what a man blinded by rage can do. Rage has no logic; it doesn't recognize reason.

On 12 August 1977, late in the evening, Machhi Singh and eleven of his companions headed for a village near his own in Punjab. As they headed for their destination—their backs erect, their eyes reflecting their burning anger—they had just one thought: to kill.

They spared no one—men, women, children, they massacred all ruthlessly. From village to village, they continued their brutality. In the end there were 17 corpses on the ground. All of them had been killed for the simple reason that they were related to one Amar Singh and his sister, Piaro Bai.

It all began in the village of Alahi Baksh Badla, at about 8.30 p.m. It was just a day before *amavasya*, the new moon day. The sun had dipped. Darkness spread all around—and from the darkness rose Machhi Singh, a demon armed with a rifle. A lantern threw its feeble light on Amar Singh, who was sleeping with his daughter snuggled close to him.

Amar Singh heard a noise and woke up. He was already apprehensive, as a murder case was pending in a criminal court against some of his relatives. Sensing danger, he rose stealthily and hid behind the reeds. He was barefoot; his shoes lay under the cot.

Amar Singh had actually heard the heavy footsteps of Machhi Singh and his companions coming towards him. Despite the dark, he could discern the silhouettes of other houses, some thatched, some pucca. Trees swayed in the wind, and he shuddered. Maybe he had a premonition of what was to come.

Machhi Singh and his accomplices arrived, their robes flowing, armed with rifles and kirpans. They struck Amar Singh's wife, Biban Bai, with a kirpan and watched the blood gush out. Biban Bai died immediately, an expression of horror on her face. In a few minutes, a toddler's dead body clung to hers. The corpses of mother and child lay on the ground, side by side. Another blow struck a table, which landed upturned on the ground.

Machhi Singh and his friends then killed two more children sleeping on a cot nearby. Amar Singh's daughter, numb with fear, slid off and hid under the string cot. Gunshots were fired. She watched the orgy of death in a stupor. She was the one who saw the bodies of her mother and brothers fall lifeless to the ground in a pool of blood. Years later, long after she had grown up, the visions of the ghastly night would come back to her again and again. The two survivors—Amar Singh and his daughter—became crucial eyewitnesses and gave the details of the incident later.

Nine of the attackers then moved on to the next village, holding aloft their rifles and kirpans. Their hands were covered with blood, but their anger remained unabated. At around 9 or 10 p.m., they reached the house of Kehar Singh, in a village called Sowaya Rai, where they killed two women and injured another. Then they hurried to a place two furlongs away. A man, a woman, and a child were killed there, too.

This was the second round of killings. And its gory details were recounted again and again in coming years by the villagers.

But Machhi Singh did not rest. Like a sea during high tide, he roared. At a place called Kho Kunjuka he entered the house of Bishan Singh and killed the entire family.

As a lawyer with two decades of practice, most of it on the criminal side, I know that the majority of those who rot in prison are first-time offenders, usually remorseful after the crime. Machhi Singh was not one of them. He had killed many—and killed without repentance.

Next, it was the turn of Wajnar Singh and his grandson Satnam Singh, who was all of 16 years. Sabban, Wajnar Singh's wife, was sleeping in the courtyard that night. The elderly woman doted on her grandson.

Sabban saw Machhi Singh looking at her with bloodshot eyes, and recoiled with fear as he shot her husband right in front of her, injuring him severely. While Machhi

Singh was armed with a rifle, two of his brothers wielded kirpans. They stood near the feet of her grandson, Satnam, who was sleeping on a cot. The three were accompanied by Mohinder Singh and Bhajan Singh, who were also armed with a rifle and a kirpan. One of them flashed a torch at the boy. Machhi Singh glared at him and fired two shots, killing him. Mohinder Singh fired two shots at Wajnar Singh and finished him off as well. The old man and his grandson died almost immediately.

Sabban cried for help. Machhi Singh turned around. He took aim and shot at her. The bullet missed, hitting the bullock tied in the courtyard instead. The animal staggered and fell. Sabban ran to hide in the dark, desperate to shake off her pursuers.

No one came to her help. When the attackers left, she sat the whole night guarding the corpses among swarms of flies.

It was only on the next day, when he was on patrol duty, that Chowkidar Sardar Singh saw the old woman sitting near the dead bodies, looking ashen. When she saw him, Sabban let out a spine-chilling wail. The policeman walked up to her and squatted on the ground beside her. He probably understood what had occurred from the scene in front of him.

'Go, call the police,' Sardar Singh said to the weeping woman softly. His presence seemed to comfort her. The day was now bright and sunny. What a contrast to the previous night that had been dark and ghoulish! The chowkidar remained near the corpses until Sabban returned from the police station after filing a report.

The sole survivor in that family, she must have led a lonely life, waiting, all alone, for justice to be served.

To continue with the gruesome tale, Machhi Singh and his cronies reached the village of Kamrewala at 1 a.m. There they killed Mohinder Singh, Amar Singh's brother-in-law, and Piaro Bai's husband. An FIR was lodged within half an hour by Piaro Bai. The hapless woman ran to the police station, barefoot, hair loose and wild. Her only concern was to rush back to the spot where the blood-splattered body of her husband lay with the available police force.

Her husband had been sleeping on a cot, she narrated to a man in khaki rapidly. She had been sleeping on another cot along with her two children. They had a guest that night, Jaggar Singh.

A kind constable handed her a glass of water. She gulped it down and continued, 'They chatted till late at night. At around 1 a.m., someone shouted, "Oye, Mohinder!" I woke up with a start. It was such a blood-curdling voice! Five men entered our courtyard. I could recognize only Machhi Singh. He aimed at my husband and fired a shot. My husband fell down, lifeless.'

Piaro Bai sobbed as she held out her husband's blood-splattered kurta. She sat in the police jeep and took them to the scene of the crime. The woman looked on as the men in khaki moved around swiftly, observing everything. The prudent investigating officer gathered pieces of evidence—bloodstained earth and clothes—which were then sent to the laboratory for testing.

Piaro Bai and Jaggar Singh later helped in the identification of the recovered weapons, and also identified the assailants in the courtroom.

By the time Machhi Singh was done with Mohinder Singh, he was tired, though his thirst for blood was still not quenched. The five attackers now went to the house of Ujagar Singh, where his sister, Palo Bai, lay asleep. Showing no remorse, they killed her, along with four of her close relatives—her husband, Jeet Singh; father-in-law, Sahib Singh; mother-in-law, Matto Bai; and Jeet Singh's cousin, Mukhtiar Singh. In the commotion, two men hid behind the cattle nearby and somehow managed to escape unhurt.

This was around 3.30 in the morning.

Of the five that were attacked, three died immediately. Only Sahib Singh and Mukhtiar Singh died in a hospital five days later. They gave their declaration before the police and the magistrate before they passed away.

Machhi Singh's case was decided by three Supreme Court judges in 1983. Seventeen lives lost on a single night was not something one was likely to forget—ever. The enmity that had led to the mass murders, odd pieces of gathered evidence, and the deposition of the witnesses convinced the courts about the guilt of the assailants.

Justice Thakkar, delivering the judgment on behalf of the bench, said that persons like Machhi Singh should be hanged; they deserved nothing less. He observed that those who demanded an eye for an eye batted for death. The humanists, on the other hand, pressed for the other extreme—death in no case. Their argument was that life was too sacred to be taken away, even by the state. (A synthesis had emerged in Bachan Singh's case when it was decided that death should be given only in the rarest of the rare cases.)

Machhi Singh had killed innocent, helpless women, young men, and a child aged six! Keeping in mind the horrendous nature of the crime, the Supreme Court refused to convert the death penalty into life imprisonment. However, certain other guidelines were laid down.

By the time Machhi Singh's case was heard, the court believed that death should be awarded only when the murder was grotesque, diabolical, and shocked the community. For example, when the house of the victim was set on fire to roast him alive; when the victim was inhumanly tortured and killed; or when the body was cut into pieces.

Then there were cases that showed a depraved mind, for instance, when a man killed for money. It included several cases in which children were killed for ransom. Or when some one killed to grab the property of their ward, that is, in the case of the murder of a defenceless child by a guardian. It was established well in Machhi Singh's case that a person who killed an innocent child, a helpless woman, or a public figure deserved nothing less than death.

In my case too, it was said that the boys had chopped off the hands and legs of their victims and stuffed them in gunny bags. Some parts had been scattered in the jungle. It was with a restless mind that I turned to the next case.

Notes

1. Machhi Singh And Others vs State of Punjab (1983) 3 SCC 470.

5

SWAMY SHRADDANANDA

Another important case was that of Swamy Shraddananda, who had killed his wife, a beautiful woman with huge properties everywhere in the city of Bengaluru. There were all the elements of high drama in this case. It was the story of a man's greed, a woman's desire for a son, and a daughter's efforts to find a mother who had suddenly disappeared from the face of the Earth.

Swamy Shraddananda, alias Murli Manohar Mishra, married one Shakereh, who came from a wealthy and respectable family. Swamy Shraddananda was a cold-blooded scallywag who had no proper qualification or profession.

The granddaughter of Sir Mirza Ismail, a former dewan of the kingdom of Mysore, and the daughter of Ghulam Hussain Nawaze and Gauhar Taj Nawaze,

Shakereh held vast and valuable properties in the city. Among her various properties was a bungalow at 81, Richmond Road, constructed over nearly 38,000 square feet of land that had been given as a gift by her parents. The bungalow was huge, with tall, leafy trees all around. At night, when all the lights were switched on, it looked majestic.

Shakereh had also received a large piece of land measuring 40,000 square feet on Wellington Street as dowry at the time of her first marriage. She had earlier been married to Akbar Khaleeli, a member of the Indian Foreign Services. They had four daughters from their marriage.

Shakereh came to know about the swamy for the first time in 1983, when she visited the erstwhile Nawab of Rampur in New Delhi as Khaleeli's wife. The swamy was introduced as someone adept at managing urban estates.

Soon after, Akbar Khaleeli was posted as a diplomat to Iran. In those days, Iran was not a family station for Indian diplomats, so he went alone, leaving Shakereh behind in Bengaluru. The swamy then came to Bengaluru and started living in a part of her house.

The smooth operator that he was, the swamy discreetly began to work on Shakereh's suppressed desire for a son and convinced her that he could help her through his occult powers. Shakereh was a lonely woman—her daughters lived abroad, as did her husband—and the swamy was constantly around. Eventually, Shakereh divorced her husband. There seemed to be little resistance from her family.

Shakereh married the swamy soon afterwards. Not only did she shower her love and affection upon him but also her wealth. Her relations with her daughters and her parents continued to be as they had always been. But in her marital life, love soon started to wane, and the wealthy woman began to suspect that the swamy was nothing but a fraud.

Shakereh had married Swamy Shraddananda on 17 April 1986. They had engaged a couple, Raju and Josephine, for their household work. The couple lived in the servants' quarters of the bungalow.

At some point, the swamy got a huge pit dug just outside the bedroom he shared with his wife.

'Why do you need such a huge pit?' Shakereh asked him once.

'I want to construct a soak pit for the toilet,' her husband replied.

The bottom of the wall was knocked off so that a large box could easily slide through. Finally, a large wooden box was made, measuring 7 x 2 x 2 feet. It was brought to 81, Richmond Road and kept in the living room.

On 28 May 1991, Shakereh got up early and went to the bathroom. The swamy observed her movements stealthily. As the door clicked, the swamy rose and stirred a heavy dose of sleeping pills into her tea. Shakereh came back, drank her tea, and slipped into a deep sleep.

The same morning, Raju and Josephine had gone to the swamy after finishing their chores to ask for leave. Apparently, someone had called from Raju's village a few days ago about a death in the family. Raju also wanted to request his employer for some money.

'Wait,' the swamy said, pointing to the wooden box he had got made. 'Bring that box to the bedroom, and then you can leave.'

Raju dragged the heavy box into the bedroom and placed it at the foot of the bed where his mistress slept peacefully.

Soon after, Shakereh disappeared mysteriously. She had last met her mother, Gauhar Nawaze, on 13 April 1991. Her daughter, Sabah, had last spoken to her on 19 April, and the two servants, Raju and Josephine, had last seen her in the company of the swamy on the morning of 28 May. After that, she was not seen or heard of. She was 40 years old at that time.

Swamy Shraddananda started selling off her properties one by one. On 31 March 1992, he sold off 34 plots of land carved out of Shakereh's property to various people under registered sale deeds, using the power of attorney in his favour. He also cleared out the bank lockers taken in joint names.

When she did not hear from her mother for several days, Sabah turned impatient. Sabah used to speak to Shakereh quite frequently, and for some time now her mother had not been taking her calls. Sabah went to her mother's house on Richmond Road and rang the bell. It was answered by Swamy Shraddananda.

'Your mother is not at home,' he said, as he made way for Sabah. She brushed past him to enter the living room. 'She has gone to Kutch to attend the wedding of a wealthy diamond merchant.'

Sabah could do nothing but wait.

A week later, the swamy told Sabah that her mother was keeping a low profile as she had income-tax problems. He told her that Shakereh had actually gone to England and had herself admitted at Roosevelt Hospital.

Putting together all the resources she could, Sabah checked the patients' records at Roosevelt Hospital.

'No,' the voice at the other end said. 'No one by the name Shakereh is admitted here.'

Swamy Shraddananda had an explanation for that too. 'Your mother wants to keep her whereabouts confidential,' he said.

One day Sabah went to meet Swamy Shraddananda at a hotel in Mumbai. She was alone in the room. The swamy had gone out to attend a call. As she stooped to tie her shoelaces, she spotted her mother's passport on the floor. It showed that she had not left the country!

Immediately, Sabah lodged a missing person complaint with the police. The complaint was in her own handwriting, long, slanting, with loops. She tried to give all the details. The investigation by the Ashok Nagar Police Station did not yield any results, but Sabah's persistence paid off eventually.

Three years later, in March 1994, the Central Crime Branch, Bengaluru, took over the investigation of the case. The search for the missing woman began in earnest. Under intense interrogation, the swamy broke down.

While interrogating, working on an accused with no criminal record is easy, especially when intimidation or the third degree is used. It is more difficult when it is a dreaded criminal. Third-degree methods are not effective in cases of hardcore criminals who are inured to them, so the cops, in their attempt to find out the truth, focus on their weaknesses.

Swamy Shraddananda was not a hardcore criminal. God knows how he was made to confess. Was he given third-degree treatment? Was he tied down, had water poured down his nostrils? I am told this leaves no injury mark, but can be very painful. Or were his hands and feet tied and his soles struck with a hard rubber cane? This method can cause loss of vision, though not immediately. Or did they use one of the commonest methods: make him overeat and not allow him to sleep?

Each investigating officer has his or her own method.

After Swamy Shraddananda spilled the beans, the investigating officer obtained an exhumation order from the magistrate. They went behind the house, past the dining hall and the kitchen. The cluster of trees in the backyard formed a canopy. The spot where Shakereh lay buried was identified and marked with a chalk. The place was open to the sky, but closed on all four sides by huge walls. The floor was covered with Kadapa slabs. The large pieces of stone were removed and the cement below broken. The wooden box lay inside.

The box was dug out of the soil. It contained a mattress, a pillow, and a bed sheet. Under the mattress, they found Shakereh's skeleton, with tufts of hair around the skull. The forensic expert rearranged the bones and fixed the skull and the mandible.

'Yes,' said Gauhar Taj Nawaze. 'The rings belonged to my daughter.'

Josephine identified the gown on the skeleton as Shakereh's.

By the time the case reached the Supreme Court, Swamy Shraddananda was an old man. Perhaps he had spent those years in his cell in solitary confinement, deprived of all human contact, waiting for the gallows.

The verdict was given in 2007, by a division bench comprising Justices Sinha and Katju. Justice Sinha held that the death penalty was unique as it was irrevocable, and so it should be abolished. Keeping in mind that the swamy was an old man, over 64 years old, and had been in jail for more than 16 years, he declared that his death sentence should be converted to life imprisonment.

Justice Sinha had most of the judgments on his fingertips. Justice Katju, however, dissented. He felt that the court had no power to amend the constitution by judicial verdict. If the death penalty had to be abolished, it was for the legislature to bring about an amendment.[1]

Swamy Shraddananda's case was then referred to a three-judge bench for final adjudication. In 2008, Justice Aftab Alam, a soft-spoken judge, wrote the judgment for all the three, concurring with Justice Sinha. However, it was decided that the swamy would have to remain in prison for his entire remaining life, not for 14 or 20 years.[2]

Notes

1. Swamy Shraddananda @ Murali Manohar Mishra vs State of Karnataka (2007) 12 SCC 288.
2. Swamy Shraddananda (2) @ Murali Manohar Mishra vs State of Karnataka (2008) 13 SCC 767.

6

DHANANJOY CHATTERJEE

———

I researched some more judgments on the death penalty. Another important one concerned Dhananjoy Chatterjee, a young man of 27. Dhananjoy was born on 14 August 1965, in Kuludihi in Bankura district of West Bengal, about 200 kilometres west of Kolkata. Something else about his case caught my attention: my senior, Colin Gonsalves, had represented him before the top court.

Dhananjoy was a guard at Anand Apartment, where he had been deputed by M/s Security and Investigating Bureau. In one of the flats lived Hetal Parekh, a young girl in her teens. Dhananjoy constantly looked for opportunities to get close to her, even though he was much older, married, and had children. Every day he stood at the gate in the blazing sun, supervising entries made in the visitors' register and watched her cycling past him, ribbons in her hair, and an innocent smile on her face. He waited impatiently for her to come back from school, his face shining the moment she came into sight.

Hetal was irritated by his attention. She did not like the security guard and tried to avoid him. The more she tried to stay away, the more he chased her. 'I want to watch a movie with you,' Dhananjoy had said once as she had walked past him hurriedly.

On 2 March 1990, Hetal complained to her mother Yashomati Parekh, a middle-aged woman, that Dhananjoy teased her every day when she got back from school. Yashomati was furious. She remembered Hetal had complained about him earlier as well. Haunted by uncomfortable thoughts, she decided to talk to her husband about it. When Nagardas Parekh returned home from work, he sensed something was wrong. His wife was restless and seemed worried. When she told him about Dhananjoy, he was livid. Hetal noticed that he didn't take kindly to the man. He wanted to strangle Dhananjoy.

Nagardas Parekh left his flat seething, and pressed the lift button with force. As he stepped out on the ground floor, he called a few neighbours and told them about Dhananjoy's antics. He was so angry that he could barely speak coherently.

'Throw this man out!' he spat out. The neighbours tried to soothe him. 'He should be replaced immediately!'

The others nodded in agreement. The message was passed on to M/s Security and Investigating Bureau, and immediately a transfer order posting Dhananjoy at Paras Apartment nearby was issued by Shyam Karmakar, the proprietor of the security agency. Bijoy Thapa, a guard from Paras Apartment, was appointed in his place.

On 5 March 1990, Hetal's father and her brother, Bhawesh, left home early in the morning. It was exam time for Hetal. Bhawesh returned briefly at about 11.30 a.m. and went out again to join his father. Hetal returned from school, tired, around 1 p.m. after appearing for her exam.

Every day, Yashomati went to the Laxmi Narain temple between 5 and 5.30 in the evening. That day she left for the temple at around 5.20 p.m. 'Hetal, lock the door!' she called out as she slipped into her chappals. Though she knew Dhananjoy had been thrown out, she felt Hetal still needed to be careful. The man was capable of anything, considering the way he used to follow her day and night. Yashomati had discussed the issue with her husband at length the previous evening. 'Don't worry, the man has been thrown out,' Nagardas had reassured her. 'Hetal is safe enough.'

Despite the transfer order, Dhananjoy did not report at Paras Apartment. He still went to Anand Apartment as a guard between 6 a.m. and 2 p.m. There he met Dashrath Murmu, another security guard who was on duty. He told him he was going to flat number 3-A to make a call to his office. Dashrath Murmu simply stared as Dhananjoy walked by. He had overheard other security guards talking about Dhananjoy behind his back.

At about 6.05 p.m. Yashomati returned from the temple. As she entered the lift, she was informed by liftman Ramdhan Yadav that Dhananjoy had been to her flat to make a call. All colour drained from her face. She was so shocked that she leaned against the wall for support. The moment the lift reached her floor, she rushed to their flat and rang the bell again and again. There was no response.

In panic she raised an alarm. Eventually, the lock was broken by some servants, the liftman, and the neighbours.

Once inside, they opened the bedroom door. Hetal's body was lying on the floor. Her skirt and blouse had been pulled up, revealing her private parts. Her torn panties lay near the door. There were patches of blood near her head and close by, and blood stains on her hands, vagina, and on her clothes. They also found blood on the swing in her room.

Yashomati rushed Hetal to the doctor, only to be told that her daughter was already dead. A neighbour took the devastated woman to her flat. Someone was sent to inform Hetal's father. The body was taken back to her home, put on the bed, and covered with a sheet. At about 8.30 p.m. Nagardas returned home and informed the Bhawanipore Police Station. Sub Inspector Gurupada Som, the acting duty officer, rushed to the spot and recorded the First Information Report.

Upon searching the place, a broken chain, a cream-coloured button, Hetal's panties, and some other articles were seized and sealed in a packet once the seizure memos had been prepared. Statements of witnesses were also recorded. The police searched for further evidence.

On 12 May 1990, the police arrested Dhananjoy. After intense interrogation at the police station, a dust-laden Ricoh watch with a golden metal band was recovered from a rack in his house along with a shirt and a pair of trousers.

Dhananjoy had, however, offered an alibi. 'After my duty I went to the cinema, and later purchased some fruits for my brother's *janeyu* [sacred thread ceremony].'

There was no eyewitness to the crime. The entire case hinged on circumstantial evidence—and motive. Why did the man want to kill? There was ample motive. The judges observed that the girl was constantly teased when she came back from school, and a transfer order had subsequently been issued to Dhananjoy. There were 21 injuries on Hetal's body. All telltale signs of rape were present. As per the report provided by the senior scientific officer-cum-assistant chemical examiner of the Forensic Science Laboratory, semen had been found on Hetal's panties and pubic hair. The examination of clothes and private parts is crucial in a rape case.

The second guard, an important witness who had seen Dhananjoy walking towards Hetal's flat, stated that the accused had been wearing a cream shirt and grey trousers on the day she was killed.

From the evidence given by Pratha Sinha, the senior scientific officer attached to the Physics division of the Forensic Science Laboratory, Government of West Bengal, it was evident that the cream button was from the shirt recovered from Dhananjoy's house. The officer explained that all the buttons on the shirt except the third from the top, were light cream in colour and stitched in a similar pattern with an off-white thread of three-ply and Z-type twist. The third button was white in colour, stitched in a different pattern, with a milky white thread of two-ply and X-type twist. The button recovered from the site was similar to the other two buttons, he concluded.

The recovery of the broken chain from Hetal's flat also connected Dhananjoy to the crime: a man called Gauranga Chandra stated that he had gifted the chain to Dhananjoy about a month before the crime. The recovery of Yashomati's watch from Dhananjoy's house (he said it had lain in a corner, shining, and he had simply put it in his pocket) and the fact that he went absconding after the incident also went against him. Dhananjoy was caught and convicted for Hetal's murder. It was held that he resented the fact that Hetal had got him transferred and hence he had raped and killed her for revenge.

After a lot of deliberation, the top court declared on 26 March 2004 that Dhananjoy deserved nothing but death.[1] The Court refused to convert death to life imprisonment in this case. This rape of an 18-year-old innocent and defenceless girl by a security guard fell within the ambit of 'rarest of the rare', and called for capital punishment. When a protector harmed the very person he was supposed to protect, the crime could not be more heinous. The verdict was delivered against Dhananjoy, showing absolutely no sympathy for him. The chain was complete, the judges said, and though no one actually saw him kill Hetal, the evidence collected proved that he was the one who had killed her.

Dhananjoy was in Alipore jail when the news reached him that the president of India had rejected his mercy plea.

The hangman, Nata Mullick, fainted after he hanged Dhananjoy in 2004, and took retirement from his job. According to the guards, Dhananjoy spent a sleepless night before his execution and refused food. He kept muttering, 'I am innocent,' as he walked up to the gallows. 'In my next birth I will be born a rich man. Then they will not hang me.'

Dhananjoy's family had sold all their property to defend him, and his death left them in penury. Their private grief was turned into a public spectacle. There was deathly silence in his village. No one was allowed to enter or leave it. Dhananjoy's family did not come to collect his body for cremation.

Dhananjoy Chatterjee's name had echoed against the walls of the judicial system for 14 long years. His death sentence became one of the most controversial cases of capital punishment in the history of Indian judiciary. Human rights organizations protested that the death penalty was too harsh in India's imperfect judicial system, where the poor were hanged and the rich got away. People took to the streets in Kolkata, protesting that Dhananjoy did not get a fair trial.

The case put an end to the near moratorium on executions in India.

Note

1. Dhananjoy Chatterjee alias Dhana vs State of West Bengal (1994) 2 SCC 220.

7

THE MUMBAI BOMB BLASTS

———

As I went through these cases, I noticed that the courts were getting mellower, and a death sentence was awarded only in exceptional cases. In fact, the higher courts were more liberal—or perhaps more circumspect. One of the cases my senior and I cited during our arguments was that of the Mumbai bomb blasts in 1993 in which, except for Yakub Memon, none of the other accused were awarded death.

On 12 March 1993, there was a series of bomb blasts in Mumbai, and the financial capital of the country grappled with attacks of terror. Dawood Ibrahim, Tiger Memon, and their cronies wanted to avenge the demolition of Babri Masjid, the mosque with triple domes on Ramkot Hill in Ayodhya, and the suffering of the Muslims in one of the bloodiest communal riots that had consequently erupted the year before.

Dawood Ibrahim and Tiger Memon are familiar names in the Mumbai underworld. Known for extortion and smuggling goods in the country, the two left a blaze of terror that painted the city with blood and gore. As the bombs exploded one after the other in Zaveri Bazaar, hotels (Sea Rock, Juhu Centaur, and Airport Centaur), and the Stock Exchange, the city of Mumbai trembled with shock and fear. The air was thick with smoke, and bodies and body parts were strewn on several roads. Many Mumbaikars died that day. The blasts changed the communal fabric of the city for the worse, and led to a kind of ghettoization of Muslims.

The Babri Masjid in Ayodhya, a Muslim shrine, was brought down on 6 December 1992 by Hindu *karsevaks* (volunteers) when, backed by some politicians, they decided to 'reclaim' Ram Janmabhoomi—the land considered to be Ram's birthplace—from the Muslims.

It was believed that during the Mughal invasion in the sixteenth century, Mir Baqi, a Mughal general, tore down a Ram temple at the site in order to construct a mosque there. For centuries the place had been a sacred site for all Muslims. Then, in 1949, some members of the Hindu Mahasabha reinstated idols of Ram inside the mosque. The Muslims saw red, and it led to communal riots in which Hindus retaliated. Over the years, the Vishva Hindu Parishad (VHP) firmed up their resolve to reclaim the land and rebuild a Ram temple. This was in the 1980s, and their cause was supported by the Bharatiya Janata Party (BJP). In 1986, following the ruling of the court, Hindus were once again granted access to the site for worship.

Things came to a head soon enough. In September 1990, BJP leader L.K. Advani led a *rath yatra* (a rally) for the Ram

Mandir movement, which culminated into a full-fledged campaign by 1992—and on 6 December the same year, some supporters of the VHP and Rashtriya Swawamsevak Sangh could be seen at the mosque in Ayodhya. There were over 100,000 of them. Politicians such as L.K. Advani, Murali Manohar Joshi, and Uma Bharti apparently gave incendiary speeches, which has invited flak from liberals, intellectuals, and the like for years afterwards.

Not many of those present could have imagined the consequences their bravado would eventually lead to. Towards the afternoon the crowd, armed with pickaxes, hammers, and such, turned restless. One thing led to another. Constant provocative speeches managed to instigate the crowd that then began sloganeering.

That was also a day when the presence or absence of the police on site meant nothing. Eventually, a young man carrying a saffron flag was spotted climbing onto the mosque. That was the moment when an unprecedented frenzy began. The mob started to tear down the heavy sixteenth-century structure; the karsevaks led the manic destruction. Some claim the police were secretly pleased and were only pretending to call the karsevaks off. Nobody knows whether the whole rampage was really carried out with the collusion of the police. Within hours, the triple domes of the mosque on Ramkot Hill were pulled down to the ground. The largest lay like a turban fallen off a giant's head. The birthplace of Ram Lalla was freed!

Once the mosque lay demolished, the attackers roamed the city with gleaming knives and cans full of kerosene. It was a free-for-all. Men and women looked at one another with distrust, avoiding those they had known for years. Others were scared of stepping out of the safety of their homes. Children no longer played outside, and playgrounds, normally filled with their laughter, fell eerily silent. Local trains, which would otherwise have been packed, ran without any passengers.

Several leaders of the BJP landed up in custody. Months of communal riots followed this shameful historical incident, and its consequences were spread far and wide— one of them being the 1993 Mumbai bomb blasts.

I talked to a local lawyer from Mumbai who filed a case against an order of the Bombay High Court and came to the Supreme Court when the case was listed for arguments. He provided details about what had happened after the demolition of the Masjid.

'There was a cluster of chawls,' he said, 'and in one particular incident, they burnt the entire row of houses and the inmates were roasted alive! I could hear their shrieks as the leaping flames engulfed them.'

In true Bollywood style, revenge and retribution for the Ayodhya episode came in the shape of Dawood Ibrahim, Tiger Memon, and their cronies, in 1993. Violence begets violence; there could hardly be another example that demonstrates the fact so powerfully.

Dawood Ibrahim was the top don and leader of the organized crime syndicate called D-Company in Mumbai. Wanted not just by the Indian police but by Interpol, his name was associated with cases of cheating and criminal conspiracy. He was also known to maintain links with the Al Qaeda and Osama Bin Laden, and was the third name on *Forbes'* The World's Most Wanted Fugitives list of 2011.

A man with thick-set eyebrows and a thick moustache, Ibrahim looks more like a businessman than a dreaded criminal. Perhaps his approach to crime is the same as a businessman might have to his trade. He was the one who took it upon himself to avenge the demolition of the Ayodhya mosque on behalf of all Muslims.

Dawood Ibrahim, Tiger Memon, and their henchmen held meetings in Dubai. Some meetings were also held in Mumbai. The job was Herculean; it involved bringing huge quantities of arms and ammunitions to Mumbai, and enthusing those who would be ready to plant bombs.

On 12 March 1993, 13 bombs went off in Mumbai, killing 257 people and injuring over 700. The authorities believe that the attacks were masterminded as well as financed by Ibrahim. Apparently, the terror attack had been planned for April (and would have covered all the big cities, besides some others), but Memon felt the police had received a tip-off from his own aide, Gul Noor Mohammed Khan, and so he brought forward the assault to March. Under pressure from his family, Khan had cleverly managed to have himself arrested in another case so as to avoid being involved in the terror attacks. The attacks were supposed to occur on Shiv Jayanti, the birth anniversary of Shivaji, the historical Indian hero.

After the arms were brought in, Memon and his gang needed men to be trained to use them. So they targeted young, unemployed Muslim youth who had suffered in the communal riots or had lost families or friends during that time, and would be easy to coax. Poverty can lead to crime. The lure of quick money can be a catalyst. And here were these young boys in pajamas and skull caps being indoctrinated day and night. They were told: 'You are serving Allah and will go to *jannat*—paradise—the land of beautiful gardens, orchards, and undiluted happiness, the abode of those who serve God.'

During the riots the previous year, the family members of the Memons, who lived in the Al-Hussaini building near the Mahim police station, could hear women in their neighbourhood mourning day and night. Someone had lost a son, another had lost a husband. Those burka-clad women, sitting alone, crying, gave them sleepless nights.

Between February and March 1993, Tiger Memon and Dawood Ibrahim sent some of the neighbouring Muslim boys for training to Pakistan via Dubai. They were given fake names and were taught how to handle AK-56 rifles, pistols, hand grenades, and RDX to prepare bombs. RDX, locally called *kala sona* (black gold), was the most powerful of military explosives. Tiger Memon wanted to give the boys rigorous training in handling big arms and ammunition.

To use a weapon such as an AK-56, the shooter is required to keep it moving for maximum casualties, as these weapons give no time to the opponent to react. A pistol requires a magazine with 12 or 13 cartridges at a time, and then it needs to be refilled or replenished with another magazine. The revolver has a chamber fixed to it and has six cartridges at a time. The chamber rotates automatically each time a shot is fired, and then the live cartridge takes position for the next shot. But these weapons cannot match an AK-47 or AK-56, which can fire a far higher number of shots in one round.

Did the Mumbai cops have the necessary training to deal with those handling such weapons? Officers normally handle small weapons, like pistols or revolvers, and do not practise frequently. Rapid firearms such as AK-56 are invariably handled by subordinates, who practise regularly. The boys employed by Memon practised for 10 days, which was considered enough. It is only for shooting certain targets that exhaustive practice is required, for instance, in those cases where the target is invisible, and so judgment and accuracy are needed.

Some of the training was also imparted in India, and then the tutors tried to destroy the evidence by disposing of their hand grenades at Andheri Creek on 8 March. After the training was finally over in Dubai, Tiger Memon asked all the boys to place their hands on the Holy Quran and pledge that they would keep it a secret. Like all jehadis, they were brainwashed into believing that they were serving their brothers and the great Muslim cause, that they were reserving a place for themselves in heaven.

About 20 to 80 kilograms of RDX was used, as they aimed to kill hundreds of people. Meetings were held secretly in the dark, behind closed doors. Spots were selected after great deliberation and debate, and, finally, vehicles for planting the explosives were chosen—three scooters, three commander SUVs, two Maruti Omnis, and an Ambassador. Their headquarters in India was the Al-Hussaini building in Mumbai—in the official residence of Tiger Memon and his family.

Explosives such as RDX and firearms were stored in garages owned by the Memons and their relatives. These garages and open spaces were used for making bombs at night. Between 11 and 12 March, the boys filled several suitcases with RDX and loaded them into the vehicles at Al-Hussaini. On 12 March, the bombs were planted at the selected targets in Mumbai, and they ripped the whole city apart.

There were explosions at 12 places. About 257 people died, over 700 persons were injured, and property worth

Rs 27 crore was destroyed in the process. They targeted Zaveri Bazaar, the crowded area known for its narrow lanes chock-full of jewellery shops, as they believed that the jewellers sympathized with right-wing Hindus and deserved to die. The passport office was bombed as well, and so were five-star hotels.

People ran in panic as news channels flashed images of mangled bodies. Severed limbs were strewn around the city, and bodies dripping with blood lay in the open, unclaimed and unattended. Mumbai seemed to be ravaged as if by a war. And ravaged by a war it was. Some even believed this war to be holy!

This was the first ever terrorist attack after the Second World War where RDX was used on a large scale. War, the biggest sport mankind has known, where one has the licence to kill and maim, where the act of killing is glorified.

Initially, Mumbai Police was at a complete loss. But then they discovered the maroon Maruti Omni with the RDX and seven AK-56s, and traced the vehicle to Yakub's sister-in-law, in whose name it was registered. Yakub Memon, Tiger's brother, was caught in Nepal and transported to India, though he denied all charges.

To those who knew Yakub closely, the news came as a shock. He was described as 'mild-mannered and debonair' by Chetan Mehta, his school friend and associate, with whom, after passing his chartered accountancy exam a few years previously, he had started the firm, C.C. Mehta and Memon Associates. Yakub's own firm, Tejarath International, used to export meat. Mehta found it impossible to believe that his friend and associate could be—and was taken prisoner for being—involved in such a monstrous crime.

Yakub confirmed he was Tiger's blood relative, but denied his involvement in the attacks. He brazenly refused to admit that he had financed the attacks or paid the co-accused in the case. Then he denied that the car used for the purpose had been his own. He argued that he didn't own one. When the matter of passing on explosives to Amjad Meher Baksh, supposedly his henchman, came up, Yakub responded that Baksh had been set free by the Supreme Court. He also shied away from acknowledging that he had an apartment in Al-Hussaini building where the explosives had been stored.

The case was cracked by the Mumbai police with great speed. Those cops, in their heavy boots and khaki clothes, worked with alacrity. In the days that followed, the country's top investigators climbed up and down the paan-stained stairs of the seven-storey Al-Hussaini building again and again where the Memons lived.

Once they got a lead, the police solved the case in two days. The boys were flushed out of their holes—and like rats they scurried out. They were caught with AK-56s and other weapons. Within eight months, the police completed the probe, and a 10,000-plus page charge sheet was filed against 189 accused.

In September 2006, four members of the Memon family—Yakub, Essa, Rubina, and Yusuf—were declared guilty and convicted. Suleiman, Hanifa, and Rahil, the other family members, were acquitted for lack of enough evidence against them. The former were held guilty of conspiracy and playing a role in 'acts of terror'. Yakub was also found to possess a cache of illegal arms. He was arrested by Nepal police at Kathmandu airport, and handed over to the CBI in India. He was the only one in the entire case to be awarded death.

Criminal law was set into motion. Arrests and recoveries were made. It was a case in which 123 persons were sent to trial before the special judge, Terrorism and Disruptive Activities Act (TADA) Court, out of whom 100 were convicted. Of these, 44 persons, including Dawood Ibrahim, are still absconding.

On 21 March 2013, the top court upheld the death penalty of Yakub Memon[1]—he was in a position of authority and the confessional statements of other co-accused established that he was the commander and one of the brains or 'archers' behind the whole conspiracy. Others, like an erstwhile broom seller who lived in abject penury (and for whom the only glimmer of hope was provided by the world of crime), or a female member of the Memon family who suffered from a psychiatric problem, were let off. However, they had to remain in prison for the remainder of their lives.

Yakub Memon was finally hanged in Nagpur Central Jail on 30 July 2015, amid great public furore. His hanging unleashed a fresh debate on whether the death penalty should be given at all in a civilized society. Yakub did not sleep the night before he was to be hanged, and expressed one last wish to talk to his daughter Zubeida. Hanged amid tight security, his dead body was handed over to his brother on the condition that they would not parade it in public.

While arguing our case before the Supreme Court, we brought up the issue of the Mumbai blasts. The point of raising this issue was simple. Not all the accused in my own case were 'archers', the brains behind the killings.

They were simply the 'arrows' or pawns in the entire game—and I needed to convince the court of that.

Note

1. Yakub Abdul Razak Memon vs State of Maharashtra (2013) 13 SCC 1.

8

The Law is Not Mathematics

It is easier to decide a case when there are eyewitnesses, as in Machhi Singh's case. The little girl who took refuge under the cot, or Sabban, the old lady who saw bullets pierce her husband and her grandchild, could tell the whole tale to the curious world.

Where there are no eyewitnesses, the matter becomes trickier. I remember rushing into the courtroom once with such a case. Turning over the pages of the brief, I started my argument with the words, 'My Lords, there is not a single eyewitness in the present case,' as the judges nodded and took note of the fact.

It makes a huge difference. The idea is to drive home the point that the evidence should be considered very, very carefully. No one saw the crime being committed. Hanging the accused, or even taking away his or her liberty for a couple of years, would not be justified on the basis of guesswork.

Swamy Shraddananda's case, too, was based on circumstantial evidence. I cited this judgment when I drafted my own petition. Just as it was difficult to identify the dead bodies in my case, Shakereh's body was also beyond recognition. It had decomposed. All one could see was a skeleton—a bag of bones with tufts of hair around the skull, and a soiled gown hanging over it as upon a scarecrow.

Josephine, the maid who lived with Shakereh had confirmed that it was Shakereh's gown; Gauhar Nawaze, Shakereh's mother, had claimed that the rings on the skeleton had belonged to her daughter.

But anyone could have slipped the rings onto the bony fingers of the body when no one was looking. Someone could have even dug up the box and slipped the gown over the dead body in the middle of the night when all were asleep. It is not really a difficult thing to do. Such things happen in real life.

The killers could have been the servants, Raju and Josephine. After all, Shakereh was a wealthy woman and possessed large properties. The couple could have gone to the deserted bungalow and exhumed the body. Raju may have held the bony fingers and Josephine could have silently slipped on the ring she had stolen. Maybe. It is possible. It cannot be ruled out that there could have been alternative scenarios. Maybe the swamy never killed Shakereh. Maybe, fearing the disappearance of his wife would mean the end of a luxurious lifestyle he was accustomed to (Shakereh had daughters—claimants to her vast properties from her first husband), he started selling off her properties one by one. Far-fetched, perhaps, but not impossible.

Raju and Josephine may have killed her after a heated argument, or after they had stolen expensive pieces of Shakereh's jewellery. People kill for a single gold chain... or even for a few hundred rupees.

Or, Swamy Shraddananda and the servants may have conspired together in the semi-darkness, sitting under leafy trees that stood as mute spectators. And while the swamy was caught, the others were not.

Judges are not gods, though they have been entrusted with a job that demands god-like powers. The brightest and the most well-meaning judge can make a mistake. This is what Justice Sinha meant when he said in Swamy Shraddananda's case that where the sole basis of judgment is circumstantial evidence, there are far greater chances of wrongful convictions in comparison to cases that are based on concrete proof. He had strongly advocated in Swamy Shraddananda's case that the death penalty should go; it had already been done away with in many countries.

Justice Sinha's words made perfect sense to me. My case was also based on circumstantial evidence. I emphasized this point several times over while drafting it. There wasn't a single eyewitness. At times, a watertight case against the accused can later turn out to be an instance of a perfect frame-up. Where there is no eyewitness at all—as in my case—there was obviously enough margin for error. The death penalty could not be awarded simply on the basis of circumstantial evidence. As in Swamy Shraddananda's case, no one actually *saw* the murders taking place. It was mere conjecture and shooting arrows in the dark. The opponents were just trying to put two and two together to arrive at a figure *they* wanted.

The judges in the Supreme Court are generally above sixty, with a great deal of knowledge and experience behind them. But no one is infallible. The law is not mathematics, where two and two make four. No one can say with certainty that an accused is guilty of the crime; there are multiple scenarios possible. It is all based on possibilities and probabilities. The task before the judges is much more onerous in a case where they have to take away a citizen's most fundamental right: the right to live. Two judges may hold different positions given the same set of facts.

Take the case of Dhananjoy Chatterjee. He had been in solitary confinement for 13 years. This, to my mind, was in itself a serious punishment. Section 30 of the Prisons Act, 1894, stipulates that a person sentenced to death shall be kept apart from other prisoners, with a guard to keep an eye on him or her, day and night.

Justice Sathasivam, the erstwhile Chief Justice of India, and the one who heard my case, expressed his anguish over the inhuman aspect of solitary confinement and observed that it had the severest impact. To island a human being, to keep them incommunicado from their fellows, was the story of the Andamans under the British, of Napoleon in St Helena. Dhananjoy had already died a thousand times before he was finally hanged, for he had been on death row for more than a decade.

Why was Dhananjoy hanged? His case had all the mitigating factors: he was young and poor. His case was based on circumstantial evidence. He may well have been framed. His behaviour in jail did not show he was a hardened criminal, yet he was kept in isolation for years. It is debatable whether the number of rapes went down in the country after he was hanged.

Many, like me, feel that the death sentence should be done away with altogether. Two wrongs do not make a right. Two deaths do not restore a life. Young hearts are impressionable and capable of change. Sceptics might shake their head, but Indian history is witness to several such cases. So many enlightened sages were once robbers, murderers, or miscreants. But something inside them snapped someday, and they had a change of heart. Look at what war and violence did to Ashoka.

If we robbed these four young misguided boys of their lives, we would be obliterating this chance, this possibility of realization and reform completely, no matter how slight or delayed it might be. Do we really have the right to do that to another human being?

The high court judgment in my case ran to about 300 pages, as they re-examined the evidence of the witnesses at length.

'The prosecution has proved its case beyond doubt,' the high court judge held. The boys had showed no mercy even to defenceless children. According to the judge, they deserved nothing short of death. 'I have seen the faces of the boys,' he observed, 'and they appear to be beyond reform.'

'No!' we argued vehemently. They were mistaken. The boys could feel the noose tightening around their throats. They were, in reality, trembling like leaves within, while they put up a brave front before the court. Perhaps they were criminals, but they needed some consideration nonetheless.

9

Bodies on the Hillock

Now, the facts of my case. A criminal case is nothing but facts. The three bags that came to me from the Supreme Court Legal Aid Services were crammed with papers that furnished all the details: the charges framed, the statements of the boys, the deposition of each witness, including the examination and the cross-examination in court, and the judgments of the two lower courts.

I started going through each scrap of paper carefully, especially marking the documents that would help me prove that the four boys were innocent, possibly framed by the cops who were anxious to establish that they had solved the mystery of the 10 dead bodies found on the plateau of Sindhudurg, Maharashtra, on 20 December 2003.

The state of Maharashtra has a series of tablelands or highland regions. An aerial view would show raised areas and hillocks with patches of green and streams of water. Much of the state consists of the high Deccan plateau, which is separated from the coastline by the ghats, a succession of steep hills crowned by some medieval forts. The jungles are extensive, with tall bamboo shoots, arching trees, and shorter bushes. The district of Sindhudurg is bordered by the Arabian Sea on the west and the Sahyadri range on the east. It has a marvellous seashore and is known for great scenic beauty. It was in one of these thick jungles in the Nandos plateau that the bodies were found.

On 20 December 2003, the superintendent of police (SP), Sindhudurg, Oros, received an anonymous call informing him about dead bodies lying abandoned in that area. The SP's message was passed on to his juniors. The station-in-charge was on patrol duty. He reported the discovery of the bodies by wireless communication to the control room. Police Inspector (PI) Rajendra Mungekar, who had been on the plateau of Nandos right from the evening of 12 December, rushed to the spot with some other cops.

At around 7.30 p.m., the police squad and a few villagers climbed up to the spot and commenced the search. They moved around groping in the dark and discovered the dead body of a male with the left hand and the right leg missing. It was found in a rocky area, about 30 feet below the plateau, lying in an inclined position with the lower jaw turned towards the right side, showing a crack on the left cheek. One eye was closed, while the other was half open. There was a twine around the waist.

The cops looked for more bodies. Most trees stood so high that you had to crane your neck to look at the top. Thin, snake-like vines sprang up from the earth in almost all directions. Dry leaves crumpled under their shoes as they struggled to remove the undergrowth with the help of obliging villagers who barely spoke out of shock. Who had done this? And so close to their own village! They began speaking in hushed tones.

It was a rocky area, and the land sloped gradually. Some village folk strayed ahead. About 20 feet away from the first discovery lay another body—that of a female. The villagers stared at it fearfully. It was decomposed, naked, and headless. The swollen breasts stood out. Some of the men shook their heads. One ran back to inform the cops. It was awkward that the woman was naked, and her flesh half-eaten by the predators in the jungle.

PI Mungekar hurried on, using his stick to get past the vegetation. He stooped to look at the body of the woman in the torch light. Who was she? And why did someone want to kill her? Had she been assaulted before her limbs were chopped off?

Around 20 feet from where she lay they came across black plaited hair. In the darkness it looked like a horse's tail—sticky, with a hair clip clinging to it. There was also a human skull near the hair—probably the scalp of the unfortunate woman.

The cops scanned the area the whole night, hunting for more bodies. They were assisted by the villagers, their torches and lamps occasionally throwing light on a half-eaten leg, a severed palm, or a missing finger. While the world slept, the police and the villagers toiled amid the thick wilderness and the rocks underneath.

Towards morning, some labourers were engaged to clear the road leading up to the plateau. Brambles and bushes were cut; the maze of wild weeds was removed. Seven dead bodies had been found during the night. They lay side by side. The cops and the villagers moved from one place to another, pointing out anything they found out of place. A foul smell came from the northern side of the plateau—the stink of rotting flesh. No one had slept that night. They had huddled together and spoken in whispers until the sun slowly rose from the horizon, its slanting rays illuminating the plateau once more. It was a bright day. Searching became easier, and soon they found yet another body, spilling out of gunny bags. It was labelled as dead body number 8 and ferried to the hospital.

The team also spotted a diary splattered with blood. Nestled behind a rock, it was fluttering in the wind, its pages still intact. A villager bent down to retrieve it. This diary later provided vital clues and helped the police in cracking the case. Vinayak Chavan, the brother of Dadasaheb Chavan, one of those killed, identified it with a sense of resignation, 'Yes, it belonged to my brother.'

The superintendent and the assistant superintendent of police reached the spot exactly at 9 a.m. PI Mungekar could barely stand. His legs ached terribly, and his eyes were heavy with sleep.

Search operations continued. The police and the villagers combed the entire expanse and recovered things like the buckle of a belt, a ball point pen, a safety pin, and a 25-paise coin— all half burnt. They also found the partly burnt remains of a yellow sari.

'Perhaps, the naked woman whose head had been chopped off was wearing this when she came here,' one of the villagers remarked as he stared at the fabric that was slightly tattered at the edges.

There were blood marks everywhere. By and by, a soiled shirt was found with dried blood on it, along with a pair of chappals. The bag also contained a ball of coir, brass caps, a lead ball, and a plastic case. Clumps of ordinary soil and soil mixed with blood were collected from the spot, labelled, and put away in separate packets.

They also recovered dead body number 9. It had on yellow underwear and a talisman around the neck in black twine. One could see the broken skull in the broad daylight. It seemed as if someone had struck a blow on the head. The face was smashed beyond recognition. A hacksaw blade, a saw for cutting metal, was found concealed under a big stone close by.

After 36 hours of death, the neck, the abdomen, the shoulders, and the head of a dead body begin to turn a discoloured green. This is followed by bloating. The eyes and the tongue protrude as the gas inside pushes them out. Tissues break open and release gas and other fluids. The body then shrivels into a dark, leathery parchment. The bodies recovered from the plateau of Nandos looked like that. Decomposition was at an advanced stage. At times, the forensic experts did not even have any skin available to them for examination.

Who could have done this?

A villager called Ravindra then happened to remember that another dead body had been recovered earlier on 27 September at around 11.30 a.m. from Salel Nagarbhat nearby. 'Sambhaji Pofale, another villager, and I noticed it floating in the stream, bloated and disfigured,' he told the cops. 'We were horrified to see the unknown man drifting away with the water like that. The cops were called in, and one of them, an able swimmer, fished the body out. I stepped aside, and he dragged it to a gunny bag and put it inside. The dead man wore blue shorts. The earlobes and the lips were missing, probably nibbled away by the fish. And then we buried it, as no one came forward to claim it.'

The police suspected that there may have been a connection between the single body discovered then and the slew of bodies that had come to the fore now. V.K. Sawant, another policeman, was then sent to the Salel Nagarbhat burial ground on Kasal Malwan Road, which was about 5 kilometres from Katta. The spot was covered with pebbles and thorny bushes. Some of the villagers went with him and watched as the men dug up the ground with a shovel and pulled out a skeleton. The skull was detached from the body. A bit of flesh stuck to the chest and back, and some hair hung over the head. The body had been exhumed in the presence of the executive magistrate and the recovery witnesses, and was later handed over to Assistant Sub-Inspector Gosavi from Katta outpost, around 3.30 p.m. A label was then stuck to it: dead body number 10.

10

GUNS, KNIVES, AND SWORDS

————

The blood-splattered diary proved to be the guiding light and led to major developments in the investigation. On 21 December 2003, Vinayak Chavan (the brother of Dadasaheb Chavan, whose body had been found in Sindhudurg) learnt from his friend, Arjun Jadhav, that the Sindhudurg Police Station had made a telephone call about the recovery of some dead bodies. Along with them, they had discovered a telephone diary in which his brother's name had been mentioned. Though Vinayak Chavan set out for Sindhudurg in a private car, along with his wife immediately, he managed to see the diary only later—on 23 December. Slightly bigger than a cigarette packet, the diary had been recovered by Subhash Thombre, a cop. According to the report of the chemical analyser, there were bloodstains on it.

The diary contained the telephone numbers of friends and relatives of Dadasaheb Chavan. There was another phone number—that of Ramesh, whom I was defending in the case. From 26 December 2003 onwards, the SP of Sindhudurg started contacting all the people whose names had been mentioned in the little booklet.

The deputy superintendent of police (DSP), CID (Crime) collected the list of missing persons from the entire state of Maharashtra. On the basis of the missing-person complaints recorded at some police stations, such as Vashi, Badlapur, and Wai, the investigators managed to identify the dead and also received information that my clients had contacted them or their relatives somewhere around the time of the murders.

A missing-person report had been lodged at Vashi Police Station regarding Kerubhai Mali and his family. Mali used to be a resident of Navi Mumbai, engaged in the wholesale business of fruits. He had two shops at Agricultural Produce Market Committee complex in Vashi. One was in his name and the other was in the name of his wife, Anita. The fruit merchant had apparently been facing financial problems. Their two children, Rajesh and Sanjay, were also missing.

'The fruit merchant was in debt,' the DSP said, relieved that he had made some breakthrough, 'and his extended family thought he was hiding to avoid his creditors...I did not make further enquiries at the time, but then I heard that Kerubhai Mali had two school-going kids. I came to know that Vashi police had asked Ramesh—a resident of Mumbai—about the missing man and his family. Ramesh was from Sindhudurg district and had apparently been in constant touch with the victim before he disappeared along with his family.'

The cops had a vital clue now. They suspected that some way or the other, Ramesh was associated with the crime.

Ramesh was a young man, around 29. His father was an alcoholic, and owned some land. His mother, Laxmibai, suffered from attacks of epilepsy. He had hardly had a happy childhood.

Both Ramesh and his younger brother used to live with their uncle Suryakant Anand Korgaonkar and his family in a village a few kilometres away from where the bodies had been recovered. Ramesh had studied up to the fifth grade, and assisted his uncle in his work. As a child, he would take their cattle to the plateau deep inside the jungle to graze. He would sit on a big rock, chewing a juicy stem he had plucked, keeping an eye on the livestock. And once the cattle were done, he would trudge back home through the narrow, dusty lane, past the school and the gram panchayat. He could walk the kaccha road with his eyes shut.

In 1995, Ramesh requested Satish Korgaonkar, another one of his uncles, to take him to Mumbai along with him. Once in Mumbai, he took to plying an autorickshaw in Borivali after obtaining a valid licence. He married Sujata More, the daughter of a police constable. And later he also married Sonali, his second wife, in Mumbai. They had no children. When the investigation began, he was back in Nandos to attend his father's funeral.

In the first week of December 2003, Satish received a call from Sujata, Ramesh's first wife, informing him that he had been arrested by the Vashi police. Ramesh was released on 9 December when his father died. On 18 December, Satish, along with his family and Sonali, left Mumbai for Nandos to attend the *shraadh* ceremony of Ramesh's father. Ramesh was arrested again on 22 December. Both his uncles, Suryakant and Satish, were present when the police came at 7.30 p.m. A heavily built cop stood at their entrance. 'Ramesh!' he hollered.

Panicking, Ramesh tried to hide in the loft.

'Ramesh!' Satish threw an exasperated look at him. 'Why are you hiding?'

'*Mama*, promise to help me out if anything happens to me,' Ramesh begged his uncle.

Satish felt that his nephew's behaviour was odd.

The cops arrested Ramesh, tied his hands with a thick rope, and took him away. They say it is usually the lower subordinates in the police hierarchy who torture a suspect during interrogation to try and make some breakthrough. Ramesh was beaten mercilessly over and over again. His face was swollen, and he limped when he went to make the recoveries for the police.

In India, torture is a routine method during interrogation: the cops punch, kick, or strike the suspect with their hands to make him talk. They also use the Reid method—questioning the accused in a dingy room, with one officer playing the good cop and another the bad cop. If you spill the beans the ordeal will soon be over, assures the good cop. The bad cop, on the other hand, tries to terrify the suspect. They keep their victim in isolation in a windowless interrogation room. The idea is to put the suspect under immense pressure and crush their morale.

The police took Ramesh and the *panchas* in a police vehicle after he had been made to confess. Panchas are the recovery witnesses. They are supposed to be independent attesters of the fact that recoveries were really made, though in real life the panchas sign on dotted lines and do as they are directed by the cops. Ironically, an independent witness is associated with the recovery of weapons of offence, or articles related to the crime, to confirm that the police did not concoct the evidence.

The prosecution said that Ramesh had confessed during interrogation, that in October 2003, when it was time to harvest the paddy, he had gone to see Tanaji Gawade, an arms seller. Gawade was a close friend of Ramesh's uncle Suryakant. Ramesh was said to have visited his house in the evening and bought two guns from him, along with a belt. The parts of the guns had then been dismantled.

* * *

'You can disassemble the parts and realign them later,' Gawade had explained to Ramesh, demonstrating the process to him. 'This is how you *should* do it. Take care that it is done the proper way...But why do you want to know this, anyway? What do you want with a gun?'

'I want to hunt,' Ramesh had told him. 'Sparrows and small birds.'

* * *

The police had decided to lay their hands on the arms seller to extract the truth from him. They crossed the fields to reach Gawade's house. It was an old, dilapidated structure, with plaster peeling off and the rooms constructed in an unplanned way. It was located about 25 kilometres from the police station and took them 45 minutes to reach.

'I sold the gun to him,' the arms seller said simply when the police asked him about Ramesh.

'Can you show us the weapon?' the cop asked.

The latter led them towards a road about half a kilometre from the house. The gun was hidden under some dry leaves near a cashew tree. It was a big tree, with its leafy branches spread out. The arms seller removed the leaves with his big hands and produced the gun—a country-made muzzle loader, 46 inches long.

As the cops sat taking measurements, Ramesh squatted on the ground and watched them silently. The police seized it. Ramesh disclosed the names of his associates much later. With his face swollen from beatings, it had been an effort for him to name the three others who had been involved in the crime: Karim, Salim, and Shyam.

All the four boys lived in Mumbai. Karim and Salim were cousins. Karim was fat, and the most soft-hearted of the four. He ran a ration shop in Mumbai. Salim, fairer, with feline eyes, was an LIC agent. Shyam worked with a private institution.

* * *

The prosecution claimed that in the beginning the boys did not kill; they just duped people. Ramesh was the kingpin. Together, they had managed to swindle a few people by pretending that Ramesh had supernatural powers that would multiply profits and enlarge one's coffers. Among the people they had deceived was one Aijaz, a businessman who had suffered huge losses. Someone told him about 'Ramesh Baba' who, with his supernatural powers, could multiply money. Aijaz then met Ramesh.

'Baba, please help me,' he pleaded. Ramesh Baba provided a glimmer of hope to him. Aijaz gave him

Rs 1.2 lakh wrapped in a cloth in return for the assurance that his money would multiply in a certain span of time. Nothing of the sort happened, and Aijaz stared with dismay when all he got after the term expired were some dried rose petals wrapped in paper!

There were others like Aijaz. Soon, Ramesh came to be known as a cheat and a scallywag. Other victims like Aijaz, who had been duped by Ramesh and his cronies, started looking for him.

At this point, Ramesh changed his modus operandi. He resorted to killing his victims once he was done. The gullible businessmen who looked to him with hope were asked to come to the plateau of Nandos with sacks full of rose petals and incense sticks. The boys ensured that the victims came by public transport. Salim, the boy with innocent looks, was entrusted with the job of bringing them over. He'd book them into hotels or lodges close to the plateau and take them from there to the plateau.

At the beginning of the ritual, Ramesh spread a plastic sheet on the floor and sprinkled rose petals on it. The naive victims watched with anticipation, their eyes closed, hands folded. The boys would put their bags in a corner. Nobody knew what the protruding shapes in the bags were. They could not have imagined that they were guns or knives.

The boys would smile warmly, encouraging the victims to dream of riches about to fall in to their lap. When they had robbed them, they would murder their victims.

This was the prosecution's theory, and they stuck to it.

In the presence of the panch witnesses the cops had seized two bamboo sticks, a plastic sheet, dried petals of rose flowers, and some incense sticks—tools used by the boys to show magic to their clients on the plateau. The

SP sent a team to catch hold of the other accused. On the basis of the disclosures made by Ramesh, Karim was caught. He had been reluctant to join the gang right from the beginning. He was poor. He was gentle. I read in the evidence that after he (allegedly) killed for the first time, he had to be taken to a doctor—Dr Rajendra Rane. He was so upset that he ran a high temperature.

After Karim was caught, he confessed to killing all those whose bodies had been found on the plateau. They had used a knife for the task. He was ready to take the cops to the place where he had hidden the weapon. The men travelled with Karim in two vehicles to the site of the murders. The path leading up to the plateau had curves, and when driving became difficult, they jumped off and walked in single file. The road was steep. Karim walked slowly, his head bowed. He led the party to some bushes on the slope of the hills and stopped at one of them. It was a small one, not easily visible. The thick, drooping branches had kept the weapon well concealed below. The leaves rustled as he groped the spot with his hands. After a few minutes, he pulled out a knife. Traces of dry blood were still visible on its iron blade. It had a wooden handle with red and green rings. It was seized and sealed.

The police also went to Suryakant's house. Ramesh climbed up to the wooden loft in his room. With one foot in the loft and the other dangling in the air, he pulled out a sword with an iron blade and a wooden handle, measuring 75–80 centimetres. The blade of the sword was slightly blunted but had a pointed tip. Ramesh gripped the wall firmly with one hand and climbed down slowly with the weapon clutched in the other. It was wrapped with paper and the twine around it was sealed at the knot.

And then Ramesh took them and his uncle to a spot at the base of the hill. Weapons were drawn out from a gap between two stones. He cringed as a muzzle loader gun was recovered, concealed beneath a blackberry bush, under a cashew tree. A part of the barrel connected to its butt with a belt was also recovered. The butt had a trigger and the cock of a gun, as well as a brass plate. There was a shortened gun with a barrel joined to a butt; it formed a complete gun when the butt was joined to the barrel with a belt. Twine was fixed around the articles and a seal was fixed on the trigger, the cock, and at the end of the barrel. A single *panchnama* of the seizure of the sword and the parts of guns was prepared later. There were two guns in all. Both were aligned.

Ramesh's uncle, Suryakant, was arrested on 28 December 2003. After all, the recoveries had been made from his house. His involvement in the gruesome killings had to be investigated. A rustic villager with a slow wit, he was fearful of the cops. Smita, his wife, was asked to come to the police station.

Salim was also arrested. The allegation against him was that he had brought gullible businessmen to the plateau of Nandos with an assurance that once they reached their destination, money would be showered on them by magic, which they could carry back in large gunny bags. He had brought the victims to the hillock, it was alleged, and stayed with them in lodges and hotels during the period of transit. He had also signed on different registers under fake names.

Salim was brought from the Kundal Police Station to the Katta outpost. He disclosed the place where he had hidden his clothes. He took the police team to Suryakant's house. There he produced a bag containing a windcheater, two pairs of shorts, and two shirts.

I did not meet any of the boys I defended in the Supreme Court. I knew they were in a jail in Nagpur. Colin Gonsalves, the senior lawyer, did suggest that we go and meet them. At times, he said, the lawyer learnt a lot about a case after meeting the accused—things he would not have known or understood in detail otherwise. Unfortunately, I could not make it.

I thought about the boys many a time, though. I saw a photograph of Salim brought by his brother, the one who came to meet me in Library No. 2 of the Supreme Court when I sat there busily brushing up on the main points to be argued. He had just barged into the library. I looked up, slightly unhappy, for I was reading the evidence of an important witness. One of Shyam's brothers had also come with him. Both the lower courts wanted to hang his brother, and he had not come with much hope to the top court. 'Our mother died last year,' he said, his eyes moist. 'She could not bear the shock.'

All the four accused had been arrested. Four policemen were instructed to take charge of the boys. 'Keep them in four different cells on different floors,' the investigating officer, Mr Prabhukhanolkar, ordered them.

The boys had lost their freedom. They could no longer roam around freely on the streets. The heavily guarded walls of the jail now stood between them and the outside world. They were finally shifted to the death row cells— isolated enclosures near the gallows which, of course, the boys could not see because of the huge walls. They were deprived of all human contact. Their days were endless as they stared blankly at the walls and the ceiling above.

II

At the Supreme Court

———

The case reached the top court in 2012, after about a decade. When a copy of the judgment of the trial court and other papers came to me in single space, I knew I would have to get them typed in double space. In the Supreme Court, every bit of paper has to be filed in double space, for the judges are old, generally over 60, and a larger font and double-spacing makes it easier for them to read. Or, I had the option of seeking concession and filing the papers as they came to me. The typing was neat. Getting the whole document re-typed would have meant gross delay. In a death penalty matter, every day's delay has to be explained—not that it doesn't have to be explained in other cases, but a death penalty case stands on a different footing.

I read the papers carefully, at times sitting up late at night when it was eerily silent. It took several days of hard work. My eyes were exhausted from spending long hours at the desk. After reading for a few hours, I neatly marked the portions I intended to attack. Breaks were short, almost non-existent. At times I would get up early in the morning and start reading. Even as a student, I had always found that studying in the morning hours helped. It was easier to concentrate. I started drafting a synopsis and a list of dates, keying in words attacking the judgments of the lower courts, showing the flaws and the reason why the top court needed to interfere. I had prepared elaborate notes, yet I feared I may have missed some point.

It was a case of 10 murders with four boys on death row. The prosecution had done a great job, I had to admit. My eyes were glued to the computer. It was almost midnight and I had hardly finished half of the work, with constant distractions from my son and daughter vying for my attention. I scanned my notes once again and resumed drafting. As I read the contents of the cross-examination, I was impressed. The foundation of a case is laid in the lower court, and I admired the professionalism with which the defence lawyer had worked, trying to put doubts in the mind of the trial judge. It was certainly a difficult case. Both the lower courts had awarded the death penalty, and there was formidable evidence against the boys. Not one, not two witnesses, but 128!

The trial judge had said of the boys, 'They are a threat to the society. A lesser punishment would be totally inadequate.'

I imagined the boys' bodies dangling from the noose.

Judges are more liberal nowadays, especially when it comes to sentencing. The maximum sentence in a murder case is the death penalty, while the minimum is life imprisonment. In India, a death sentence was a routine punishment earlier, but post *Bachan Singh*, it is awarded only in the rarest of rare cases. Are we inching closer to the abolition of the death penalty? Earlier, the guilty were either hanged or transported for life, but after an amendment in the Indian Penal Code, which came into effect from 1 January 1956, the words 'transportation for life' were substituted with 'imprisonment for life'. Transportation for life means sending a convict into exile, and was a form of punishment for certain crimes set by the East India Company.

I wanted the top court to convert the sentence of death to life imprisonment for my boys.

I finished drafting the petition and gave the command to print it all out. Stretching, I pushed back my chair and yawned. As sheets of paper rolled off the printer, my court clerk, Riyaz—a tall, thin man who had been with us for more than a decade—entered my office, quietly shutting the door behind him. Putting his bag on a chair, he started collecting the printed sheets. I yawned again. After all the hard work, I desperately wanted a few hours of sleep. 'It should be filed tomorrow,' I instructed him, while he stood with an oversized stapler. Looking at the thick volumes strewn on the table, he smiled. 'Ma'am, give me some time. Getting these photocopied and preparing paper books will take a while.'

'All right, but make it quick.'

The case was listed for preliminary hearing soon after it was filed in the court registry. I had just gone through the high court judgment, the synopsis, and the list of dates I had drafted. That, of course, would mean 300–400 pages altogether—though typed in double space. But reading even that would mean having no time to do other routine things like bathing, for I utilized a couple of minutes saved in reading a few more pages. I sat at my desk, preparing, reading the judgment, not even bothering to look at what lay on my plate as I ate, drank, and read some more.

Sitting at the breakfast table, I usually eat while I go over the points to be argued in court. At times, I read piecemeal—a hundred pages of the petition at night before I start yawning and feel it is time to hit the bed, maybe fifty pages after I have dropped my son off at the bus stop. If there is still more left, I read in the car on my way to court, giving strict instructions to my driver, Ballu, to switch off the music. The moment I am through, I ask him to turn on the radio. Ballu, like Riyaz, has been with us for almost a decade. If I'm still not done, I read in the court library, like the other lawyers.

That's where I was, reading, looking up occasionally to find out what was going on in the courtroom of Justice Radhakrishnan, where my case was listed. Some time later, I picked up my papers and took quick steps towards the courtroom. I did not want to miss my case.

'Issue notice,' the bench directed when the case was finally heard by the court at the preliminary stage. It was the bench of Justice Radhakrishnan and Justice Dipak Misra. Justice Radhakrishnan has now retired. Soft-spoken and patient, he was an extremely polite judge. It was a pleasure to appear before him. Justice Misra, who was the brother judge in the case, is now the chief justice of India. More popularly known as the judge who sat at 4 a.m. to hear the case as Yakub Memon's counsels made a last-ditch effort to save him from the gallows, Justice Misra was back in the courtroom at 10.30 a.m. the following day, despite the fact that he had been up for the most part of the night.

I was back in the courtroom about an hour after the two judges issued notice in my case. I ran past the lawyers— junior and senior—in the corridor, clutching the thick volumes of the book in my hands. No one was surprised. It is usual for lawyers to run when their case reaches the desk suddenly. But the reason I ran was different. I had forgotten to seek a stay on the execution! What if the boys were hanged while the petition was pending in the top court?

I barged into the room, panting.

All the cases listed before the court had been heard and the judges were about to rise. The ushers stood at the back. I was relieved that I could make it before the judges had left the courtroom and spluttered, 'My Lords, I seek stay of execution in my case. It is a death sentence matter.' The courtroom was near vacant, and my voice rang. Justice Radhakrishnan looked at me calmly as he dictated to the typist who stood in a black coat, ready to take down the order, 'On a request made by the learned counsel, we stay the execution.' The order was short and crisp.

The court also directed that the matter be listed on a non-miscellaneous day. In the Supreme Court, Mondays and Fridays are 'miscellaneous' days, when about 50 or 60 matters are listed before each bench. However, if the court feels that a certain case requires to be heard at length, it grants leave. Such matters are heard on non-miscellaneous days, or regular days. These matters are listed from Tuesday to Thursday. My case had to be heard on a non-miscellaneous day. There was a mountain of papers to be studied, and this was not possible on a miscellaneous day, when each case is heard for only a few minutes. The judges might feel—yet again—that my boys should be hanged, but not before they had heard me at length.

Records were called for from the high court. I waited for them to arrive, sending Riyaz to the Supreme Court Legal Aid office every few months to make enquiries. At times I went there myself, walking down the corridor and taking the flight of steps leading to the basement. I walked in the long corridor with rooms where the clerks of the registry sat on both the sides. 'Supreme Court Legal Aid Services' is written prominently just outside its office. There are cubicles where the clerical staff sits. Mr Barua, the superintendent—he is retired now—would be seated right in front. Mr Barua is a greying, slightly bulky man, and I would often listen with amusement as he shouted at those under him for not expediting work.

I would walk straight to his table, carrying the case numbers and the names of clients with me; the office received a lot of requests for legal aid, and correct details made searching easier. At times, I'd pull up a chair and sit down. A few minutes later, Mr Barua would look up from his work. After sympathizing with him and discussing for a while how inefficient those who worked under him were, I would come to the point. 'Have the records arrived?' Mr Barua would shake his head once his subordinates had crosschecked the status, and he would pull out long registers in which entries had been made. 'No. Not yet,' he would say.

The records from the high court reached the top court after more than a year.

Soon after they were received, the case was listed before the registrar. The registrar's court was small and crowded.

I took long strides towards the courtroom, which was adjacent to the courtroom of the chief justice. Taking the flight of steps leading up to it, I paused outside for a brief moment. I wondered if Riyaz had noted the item number of my cases correctly. To confirm, I began scanning the list of court items hung outside and entered the venue only after double-checking, and then pushed my way to the front when my case was finally called out. Some lawyers sat around, but most were on their feet as they waited their turn. The registrar—a balding man who often smiled when he spoke—asked, 'So you do not want to file any more documents in this case? Shall we list it before the court?'

I nodded. I wanted my case to be heard.

12

Burning the Midnight Oil

———

One day, immediately upon returning from my evening walk, I went straight to my office. (We have a residence-cum-office. This makes it easier to balance the house and the profession. My husband is also a lawyer in the Supreme Court and is my senior in the profession. At times, I seek his advice and guidance when I am stuck. We work together.)

As I flung the office door open, Riyaz looked up. He was holding the list of cases in his hands. 'Ma'am, your death penalty matter is listed as item 101 before the chief justice,' he said. It was on the top of the board. Untying my shoe laces hurriedly, I was at my desk in a minute, searching for the telephone number of my senior, Colin Gonsalves. He was the one representing the other two boys, Salim and Shyam. He had been engaged to argue their case in the court during the final rounds. As it turned out, when the case was finally argued I represented all four. Merits were the basis of my arguments, while arguments on sentencing were led by him.

Now, Mr Gonsalves, an alumnus of IIT Mumbai, had been attracted to law through his union work and out of his concern for human rights issues. He had started studying law at a night school in 1979, before he finally moved to the legal profession. He was the winner of the International Human Rights Award of the American Supreme Court Bar Association in 2004. He was also the founder of the Human Rights Law Network. The University of Middlesex, UK, presented the *doctor honoris causa* to him.

I wanted to speak to him before I argued my own case, so I called him up. 'Sir, can we have a conference tomorrow? The case is on the top of the board.' I got an appointment for 6.30 p.m.

I entered his office and went up a flight of stairs into a big hall with small cubicles where the lawyers sat and worked. Big posters decrying human rights violations were plastered on the walls. The senior was busy in another conference. I sat outside, brushing up my arguments, and going over the pages I wanted to show him. For a conference, a lawyer is required to be as prepared as she is in the courtroom where the arguments are made. The weapons are supplied to the senior who has to finally argue the case. In my case though, I was supposed to argue myself—at least for two of the boys. I felt shaky. This was too big for me and I wanted advice from someone who had more experience in this area. 'I don't want to mess it up,' I had told Mr Gonsalves on the phone. 'I want your guidance.'

'You shall have it,' he had said.

My turn came after 15–20 minutes.

'Let us see the charges first,' Mr Gonsalves said, as I spread my papers on his table. I had gone to the conference with papers in three bags. I bent over each, searching for the volume that contained the charges framed against the boys and the other accused—Ramesh's uncle Suryakant, the arms seller Tanaji Gawade, etc.—and then looked through the relevant papers: the accusations, the evidence of the witnesses, some important exhibits.

Trials are always held in trial courts or the lower courts. In the higher courts—the high courts and the Supreme Court—the evidence that has already been led in the lower courts is re-examined. If any flaw is detected, the higher courts interfere. The judges of the lower courts have the advantage of seeing the accused and the witnesses physically: their facial expressions, speech, etc. Based on that knowledge they try to arrive at the right conclusion while delivering their verdicts. The statements recorded in the trial courts are studied by lawyers even in the higher courts during their own arguments. These statements are very important; the entire case hinges on what the witnesses said. Lawyers on both sides try to reinforce their arguments by drawing support from what a particular witness stated at the time of trial. Though fresh evidence is not led in the Supreme Court, loopholes in the appreciation of evidence already led in the trial court can be shown. My job was to search for such loopholes and point them out to my senior.

I started with the four star prosecution witnesses: Smita Korgaonkar, Sachin Chavan, Satish Korgaonkar, and Santosh Yadav. All these witnesses were either related to

Ramesh or were known to him, and they provided vivid details of the boys who had come to stay with them before they went up the hillock to kill.

Smita, Ramesh's aunt, was Suryakant Korgaonkar's second wife. Suryakant had been arrested, and charges had been framed against him. Smita was far more educated than him. Her husband had a child from his first marriage. She had given him three more—Deepika, Trupti, and Neeraj. Her mentally ill sister-in-law, Laxmibai, and her sons, Ramesh and Sachin, stayed with them. The nephews, until they turned into adults, used to take the cattle to the plateau for grazing. She worked outside in the fields as well as indoors in the kitchen, being in charge of the vast extended family.

Smita had deposed against the boys in court. I showed her evidence to Mr Gonsalves.

'Sir, her statement before the court is full of embellishments and improvements. Her statement before the police hardly consisted of a paragraph, while in the courtroom she gave vivid details...Actually, she wanted to save her husband,' I presented the improvements to him page after page. 'There was a give and take between the police and her. They had promised to release her husband if she stated before the court what they wanted her to.'

'Let us see her statement before the police...hmm. Flag it. We will show it to the court...What about the servant who talked of swords and guns and claimed that the boys visited Suryakant Korgaonkar's house on the three dates? His evidence is damaging.' The senior had now moved on to the next star witness: Santosh Yadav. I had filed a separate volume in the Supreme Court; it contained depositions of some important witnesses. Now I looked up the index, riffling through the pages until I reached the leaf that had Santosh's evidence.

Santosh Yadav used to be a street urchin who was given shelter by Smita and Suryakant. His earliest memories were of snuggling close to his mother when he went off to sleep in the village temple they lived in. He often ran behind Suryakant's bullock cart; it was a sport he enjoyed. One day, the old man decided to adopt him. He was three years old at the time. Santosh had no clue whether his father was dead or living. And he had offered to speak up against the boys after the arrest of Suryakant.

The lower courts had believed him. He had furnished them with vivid details, accurate dates, and talked at length about the weapons that he had identified in the courtroom.

The boy had given such details! I really did not know how to counter whatever Santosh had stated, though I tried searching for some loopholes and showed them to Mr Gonsalves.

'Sir, he had stated that he desperately wanted to see his uncle free,' I said. It was a feeble attempt to break this witness.

I glanced at my watch. It was past 9 p.m. The hall outside the senior's room was empty. Except for one or two people, all had left. It was a cold night. I shivered slightly, adjusting my dress so as to cover myself fully.

Mr Gonsalves was now studying the evidence of the next star witness, Sachin Chavan, totally oblivious to the time.

We found out from the papers that Sachin was Ramesh's brother. He plied a rickshaw for a living. The two brothers had had a not-so-privileged upbringing. Neglected in their childhood by a mother who was mentally ill, and a father who was more bothered about where his next bottle of alcohol would come from, the brothers had barely received an education. They had been left to fend for themselves. At their uncle's place, they did nothing but work in the fields and graze cattle.

Sachin had claimed, during the trial, that he had transported two of the victims to the plateau in his auto rickshaw. He was ready to sacrifice his brother to save his uncle. Or had the police threatened to make him a co-accused if he did not depose against Ramesh and the other boys?

My senior read Sachin's evidence carefully. I told him that the high court had disbelieved Sachin; he had given all the wrong dates and details.

'Then we should not waste much time on him. Let us move on to the next witness,' he said, highlighting the portion where the judges had doubted this witness—page 125 of the high court judgment.

We moved on to the last star witness: Satish. He was Ramesh's uncle who stayed in Mumbai. This witness had tried to prove that Ramesh had used his ill-gotten money, after the killings, to buy assets such as a Tata Sumo car.

The boys were unfortunate. Their own kith and kin had given statements against them. The only way I could attack their depositions was by proving that they had had some ulterior motive in the conviction of the boys. The motive in the present witness's case seemed to be freedom for Suryakant Korgaonkar. Many accomplices are known to turn approvers, and this ultimately helps the cops in cracking the case. For my current case, I noted down that Ramesh's family members had spoken against Ramesh and the other boys because they wanted to free Suryakant. Otherwise, why had his bail petition been kept pending until all his close relatives had given detailed statements against the boys before the court?

I rose. It was now almost 11 p.m. I had a vague feeling that my son had gone off to sleep without eating his vegetables. At home, I saw to it that he ate properly. It was with some anxiety that I left the senior lawyer's chamber. Riyaz loaded the bags into the car, helped by Ballu. It had been a long day for them too. Soon we were on the dark, desolate streets of Delhi, pausing at some traffic lights. We passed the muddy waters of the Yamuna, and finally I reached home. It was midnight.

13

FINDING FLAWS AND LOOPHOLES

———

Nine bodies had been recovered from the hillock that night; the tenth was exhumed later on. Four bodies out of the nine seemed to be those of the Malis. The other four, the prosecution claimed, were all middle-aged men: Dada Chavan, Sanjay Gavare, Vijaysinh Dudhe, and Bala Pisal. The last two were Shankar Sarage and Hemant Thakre.

The boys, it was alleged, had killed the 10 victims in three rounds between September and November 2003. They had pocketed the money and the assets they had. Every time they had brought their victims to the hillock before killing them, Salim was with them. They stayed at lodges and hotels overnight, where the entries were made in the register either by Salim in his beautiful handwriting, or by the victims themselves. These registers were checked to confirm that the victims had really stayed at those lodges or hotels, as alleged by the police, before they had travelled to the jungles on the Nandos plateau.

Appa, a witness who claimed to have seen Salim with Dada Chavan, Sanjay Gavare, Vijaysinh Dudhe, and Vinayak 'Bala' Pisal—gullible businessmen in deep financial trouble—had worked as the manager of Pallavi Hotel on the national highway for 13 years. He had stated, during the trial, that he stayed at the hotel when it was peak time and went back to his house at Halwal during off season. He admitted that he had provided four cots to one Amit Shenoy and four others on 29 October 2003 in room no. 5. Appa identified Salim as the boy who had given his name as Amit Shenoy. 'Amit' sat in the dock at serial no. 4 and looked at him passively. When the prosecutor showed Appa the photographs, he had recognized Dada Chavan, Sanjay Gavare, Vijaysinh Dudhe, and Bala Pisal as the four who had accompanied Salim on the fateful day. All four of them had been missing for quite some time. 'They had left the very next day, on 30 October 2003, at about 9 a.m.,' Appa had concluded.

'Salim changed his name every time he came with new victims,' the additional public prosecutor had alleged when the case was heard at the trial court, 'to conceal his identity. Sometimes he was Amit and sometimes he was Samir. He would bring the victims to the plateau and then the other boys would kill them in cold blood.'

These witnesses were important, and my senior and I went through their statements carefully. They had helped in identifying the victims. They had also tried to establish that my client, Salim, had last been seen with them before they went missing. Based on what these witnesses had said, and the missing complaints filed by their relatives, the police had claimed they had identified the victims and their killers. The case was solved.

Dadasaheb, it transpired, was a resident of Pune, and had taken a loan from a local cooperative society to address his financial troubles. When his body was found on the hillock, he was wearing blue pants, a yellow shirt, and had a black thread around his waist. His body was identified by his brother, Vinayak Chavan, a little later after it was found. Its flesh was decaying by then. Vinayak also identified the diary that had been recovered earlier.

Sanjay Gavare had also been a resident of Pune. His body was identified by his wife, Jyoti Gavare, a school teacher at Akurdi, with whom he had lived for three years. She identified his clothes and the thread he wore around his waist.

Vijaysinh Dudhe, the third man in the group, was from Kadegaon, Satara. He was the son of Vinayak Anandrao Dudhe. When his body was found, he was wearing dark blue trousers with a metallic belt. The buckle of his belt was labelled 'Green World'. He wore a metal ring on his right hand and a Roboc shoe, size seven, on his left foot.

Bala Pisal was the fourth man, and he came from Kulgaon, Badlapur. He lived with his wife and son at Parigandha Apartment. He used to run a hotel in partnership with someone. When his body was recovered, he was dressed in blue trousers with a white full-sleeved shirt. There was a yellow rubber band on his left hand and a metal ring on one of the fingers of the right hand.

The last two were identified as Shankar Sarage and Hemant Thakre. It was alleged that they had stayed at Konkan Plaza Hotel on 25 September 2003, and had last been seen alive in Salim's company. And the witness who stated that was Prosecution Witness No. 15, Amit Patel, who was the son of the owner of Konkan Plaza Hotel at Kankavli. He maintained the hotel register, Exhibit 120, and indicated that the two men had come to his lodge on 25 September 2003, at about 1 a.m., and Salim was the boy who had accompanied them and signed his name as Samir Sonavane.

Shankar Sarage was a 40-year old man, slightly bald, with a grey beard. He had been an estate agent and a resident of Mangaon, about 20 kilometres from the city of Mahad. Hemant Thakre, the other businessman, had been a resident of Rajapur in the district of Ratnagiri. A small ring, strung on a thread, had been recovered from his dead body. Usha Anil Chavan, his sister, identified his body. She identified the blue shorts and sandals worn by her brother. She had said, during the trial, that her brother stayed with his wife and children in Dahisar, Mumbai. 'He loved collecting ancient coins and dried leaves, and strongly believed in charms and spells.' She had tried to explain why her brother had believed in the supernatural powers of Ramesh, who had posed as a baba capable of showering bank notes upon him.

As a defence lawyer in the top court, I had to attack the witnesses produced by the prosecution—those who had claimed to identify the victims and many others, and show that their statements suffered from serious flaws. I knew it was a difficult task, for witnesses from all over Maharashtra had come and talked at length about the murders and how the boys had been involved.

After we had worked for several hours discussing the case and exchanging ideas, Mr Gonsalves said, 'Since you have been through the papers thoroughly, you should argue on the merits of the case; I will argue on sentencing. That should be our strategy.'

'Okay,' I said.

'We need to show the top court that the boy at Mayur Lodge lied during the trial,' the senior lawyer continued, looking worried. 'If the court believes him, it will be difficult for us.'

The boy in question was Vinod Deoru Khar, a young fellow who worked at Mayur Lodge and who had been asked to come to the courtroom to confirm that Kerubhai Mali and his family had last been seen at his lodge with Salim. Coming to the courtrooms is certainly not a pleasant experience, and to give a statement against those who had allegedly killed 10 people in a horrible manner had not been easy at all.

Vinod had worked at Mayur Lodge, situated near the Saraswat Cooperative Bank, Main Bazaar Peth at Malwan, since July 2003. He had claimed that five persons had come to him on 14 November 2003.

I showed his evidence to Mr Gonsalves. 'The trial court went through it and recorded that there were erasures and overwriting in the lodge register.'

'Yes, but where is the lodge register?'

'Exhibit 113.'

'But where is it?' he demanded impatiently.

I went through the records. I could not find Exhibit 113.

'Make a note of it and get it next time...Anything else?'

'Yes...yes, sir.' There was so much more. 'The knife maker described the knife—the crime weapon—all wrong. Dr Rane, who claimed to have treated Karim at Katta, after the alleged killing, could not identify him during the test identification parade. The parts of the gun do not match.

Dr S. Pandurang, the DNA expert, has admitted that the samples sent to him were contaminated....'

I showed him page after flagged page. My senior took down notes with his head bowed.

'Sir,' I said, 'There are so many unanswered questions, so many inconsistencies. The boys cannot be hanged— *must* not be hanged! We have to do whatever it takes to point out these major faults in the case.'

Neither of us knew if the judges this time were in favour of the death penalty; if so, then to what extent? How convinced were they? And whether we had a chance at all or had already lost the battle before even beginning.

The knife maker was an important witness. I riffled through the pages and brought his evidence to my senior's notice. The man was an ironsmith. He was Prosecution Witness No. 10, and his statement was significant since he had claimed that he had made the knives for Karim, who had used them to cut up the victims. The medical report said that there were incisions on the bodies recovered. The cops had claimed that they had recovered some knives from Karim. Usually, to prove the guilt of the accused in the courtroom, the medical report and the statements of the eyewitnesses are matched. In this case, the prosecution had tried to establish guilt on the basis of the weapons recovered and the wounds found on the bodies of the victims, even though there were no eyewitnesses to the murders.

'Sir, he has given the wrong description of the knives,' I repeated, trying to make a case for my clients. Some incorrect statement made by one witness or the other could be a fresh lease of life for my boys.

We had innumerable cups of tea as we sat and discussed the task ahead. Mr Gonsalves read the evidence provided by Ramesh's brother Sachin as well as the knife maker, occasionally highlighting the portions that showed weaknesses in the prosecution's case. For a defence lawyer, studying the statement of a witness from every angle is vital, for the credibility of the witness is broken during the cross examination at the trial. Mr Gonsalves highlighted parts of the cross examination, while I took him to the relevant page numbers.

'We will have a conference again at 5.30 p.m. tomorrow.' He was tired, and so was I.

I was at my senior's office at exactly 5.30 p.m. the next day. Once again I sat outside his room in the big hall. The three bags of 'raw material' lay at my feet. At times, I would pull out a sheet or two as I revised my case. Soon a boy, probably Mr Gonsalves's clerk, came to me and said, 'Sir is calling you.'

I wished my senior a good evening as I pulled up a chair for myself. He smiled. A lady stood with a box of laddoos in her hands. It seemed she had won in a case that Mr Gonsalves had argued.

'Have a laddoo,' she smiled and pushed the box towards me. I thanked her, my mouth stuffed with the sweet.

We started with the evidence of Dr Rajendra Rane. He had been produced before the court by the prosecution to prove that he had examined and treated Karim after he had cut his finger—an injury he had received while chopping up his victims. Dr Rane's office timings were 8 a.m. to 12 p.m. and 4 p.m. to 7 p.m. Ramesh's uncle was his regular patient. Dr Rane, after going through some papers, had admitted before the court that Suryakant had indeed come to him with Karim for treatment.

There were flaws in the statement of the doctor too, which we intended to show the court when the case came up for final arguments. No doubt the two lower courts had already seen all these flaws and still decided to award death to the accused. But two courts have held differently on the same set of facts, and the attitude of the top court being more liberal, I had not lost all hope.

I also showed the statements of the forensic, the superimposition, and the DNA experts to the senior lawyer. Their statements were important since they had helped in identifying the dead bodies recovered from the plateau. In a case of circumstantial evidence, the identification of the dead body is most important. If you cannot say with certainty that a particular dead body is of that of victim A, how can you claim that the accused killed him? Assuming the boys had killed, who had they really killed? And these three experts had been introduced by the prosecution to prove just that.

I started with the evidence of the head of the forensics team, Dr Jinturkar.

After the doctors were through with the initial post-mortem of the dead bodies, they had referred these to the forensic experts. The job of a forensic expert is to analyse all the physical proof found on a victim's body. They also help in identifying the bodies and find out how they died. They study, for example, the length of the bones or the condition of the teeth, and based on this they decide the age of the victim and other physical aspects.

In this case, the bodies were decomposed and they stank horribly when they were recovered, as they had been discovered months after death. Some of them had body parts missing. Until the bodies were identified, one could not have moved on to the next step.

Dr Jinturkar had wisdom that comes with experience. He had served as a professor in forensic medicine in a government medical college and had worked in the medico-legal field for 35 years. He had handled the work assigned to him deftly. He had tried to prove that the deaths were homicidal and that the injuries on the bodies could have been caused by the weapons recovered from the boys.

The identity of the bodies had to be established somehow. The study of the skulls, thus, had relevance. In some cases, skulls had been available and studied by a superimposition expert in order to identify the bodies. Ratnaprabha Gujarathi, an MSc in Biochemistry, was Prosecution Witness No. 108. She had been asked to study the skulls discovered on the plateau and identify them. She had claimed to have studied about 180 skulls altogether. As a superimposition expert, she was required to confirm whether the skulls belonged to the people in the photographs.

I did not know what a superimposition expert did before this case came to me. So it was with interest that I read how this expert worked. I found that she superimposed and then photographed the negatives of the photographs of the supposed victims and their skulls. The photographs of the face and the skull were traced on paper. The skull was moved horizontally and vertically so as to observe anatomical markers that fitted into the outline of the photograph. The report was supposed to be positive when 12 different distances drawn on the polygon of the skull's photograph and the face in the other photograph tallied.

'Sir, the science of superimposition is more or less guesswork,' I said.

'Let us see what Dr Pandurang, the DNA expert, says,' he replied.

I took him through Dr Pandurang's evidence next. This witness had claimed to have identified the bodies after studying the blood samples of the supposed relatives of the victims. He was the senior technical examiner in the laboratory of DNA and fingerprinting services and had a Masters in Biochemistry from Osmania University.

It was quite late by the time we finished studying his evidence.

'Look,' said the older lawyer, 'we have worked hard and yet we know we are on a sticky wicket. Two courts have held against us. Witnesses from all over the state have come forward to give evidence against the boys. But there is still hope. The top court is generally more liberal than the lower courts. Let's hope the boys will not be hanged.'

He left his chamber. I smiled. I had not lost hope.

14

NOT A SINGLE EYEWITNESS, MY LORDS!

My case was finally heard in 2014, though it had been listed for preliminary hearing in 2012. It was heard by three judges: Justice P. Sathasivam, the then chief justice of India, Justice Ranjan Gogoi, then slated to become the next chief justice, in October 2018, and Justice Shiv Kirti Singh, a judge who comes from my hometown, Patna. Justice Sathasivam, a tall, mild-mannered judge, was the 40th chief justice of India. He retired in 2014. I had appeared before him earlier and was relieved that he would be hearing me, for the case was difficult, and despite the amount of hard work I had put in I was still not certain whether I would be able to do justice to it. He was polite and helpful, but I was still nervous.

Justice Gogoi, second in terms of seniority, will be the first chief justice from Northeast India. He will succeed Justice Dipak Misra. Justice Gogoi has now started heading the bench. And like Justice Sathasivam, he is known for dealing with cases quickly.

The third judge was Justice Shiv Kirti Singh, who is the grandson of the erstwhile chief justice of India, Justice B.P. Sinha. He, too, was soft-spoken.

My case was to be heard by a galaxy of judges!

I remained vigilant since things are quite unpredictable on regular days. A case may not reach the court for arguments for months, or it may reach there within half an hour of the judges assembling at 10.30 a.m. I kept an eye on the board, which showed the status of the court cases.

One day I sat in the library, drafting a new case. After setting out the facts in brief, I formulated the questions of law. Once again, I craned my neck to see what was going on in court no. 1. Case 101 was up.

I ran.

It was the court of the chief justice of India, the largest courtroom in the Supreme Court—dome-shaped, with a fluttering Tricolour at the top. Inside, gilt-edged paintings of erstwhile chief justices were hung on wood-panelled walls. There were two rows of chairs where the lawyers sat, with a passage in the middle. Litigants and law interns sat at the back in little enclosures.

Three judges were seated in a row on the dais, under bright light. There were a few more chairs at the back, to be used when a larger bench was required to hear important cases. The librarian who handed the books over to the judges, the steno typist, and the court master sat below.

I readied myself for the hearing.

'Can you tell us the facts of the case briefly?' Chief Justice Sathasivam asked me. 'Is it the Mumbai bomb blast case?'

'No,' I said. 'According to the prosecution, nine dead bodies were found on the hills of Nandos, and a tenth was exhumed later. Their deaths have been attributed to the four boys I am defending. The bodies were in a bad shape—decomposed and rotting—and modern techniques of forensic science, DNA, etc., were adopted to identify them.'

'Are you arguing for all the four?' Justice Sathasivam wanted to know.

I nodded. 'I will argue on conviction, while my senior colleague will argue on sentencing.' I glanced at Mr Gonsalves, who sat towards my left. The judges knew my senior and I had formed a team; they had often seen us discussing the case in the courtroom as we waited our turn.

'Are there eyewitnesses?'

'Not a single eyewitness, My Lords,' I said with emphasis. 'More than 100 witnesses claim to know something or the other about this case, but not one has seen my clients kill anyone...The lower courts are ready to hang the accused solely on the basis of circumstantial evidence.' I paused. 'My Lords have held in several cases, including Swamy Shraddananda's, that it is not right to hang someone when the sources of proof are not flawless.' I had quoted from this judgment copiously in the petition I had drafted.

Several bound volumes of papers filed in the Supreme Court lay before me. They were neatly flagged and had the high court and the trial court judgments and the depositions of the key witnesses I intended to attack in the top court.

I had made notes on each one of them on a blank sheet attached to them by Riyaz. Picking up a volume, I placed it carefully on the lectern. As I was flipping through its pages, I saw Mr Gonsalves leaving the courtroom quietly, his hand on the big knob as he opened the heavy door of the courtroom.

I intended to start with the star witnesses.

15

THE STAR WITNESSES

———

The volume I had chosen had the depositions of the witnesses. I started with Smita Korgaonkar, Ramesh's aunt, and read out her examination-in-chief aloud in the courtroom. The court master quietly handed over the paper books to the judges so they could follow me. In the beginning, I was soft, but grew in confidence with time.

'"Ramesh came to visit us once a year after he moved to Mumbai, during the Ganpati festival, usually held in the month of August. He visited us in May 2003 and stayed with us for about 15 days. Again, in September the same year, he and his friends came and stayed with us for about 10 days. On the 24th of that month, he arrived with Shyam unexpectedly, at around 1.30 a.m. In the morning they left for Katta in their Tata Sumo. Ramesh went to the plateau, which is at the back of our house, for hunting. He wore a blue jacket with a laced cap.

"Deepika, my daughter, had just returned home from school. She said she had seen Shyam roaming around her school, which was near the Nandos hills. I scolded her. 'Do you go to school to study or to see what others are doing?' She went away, sulking. At around 6 p.m., Ramesh left my house. The boys came back at around 9 or 9.30 p.m., fully drenched, though the skies were clear and it had not rained. They had some food and then rested. Deepika was jumping and skipping around. She asked Shyam with her hands on her hips, 'What were you doing near the hillock?'

'Which hillock? You must be mistaken,' Shyam replied, a bit nervous. He threw a furtive look at Ramesh.

'Please wash our clothes,' Ramesh cut in, changing the subject.

"I refused, saying I would do it in the morning. I was busy cooking. Then they drank beer on the rooftop. I turned up my nose at them, unable to stand the smell. Oblivious to my reaction, they drank, laughed, and slapped each other's backs, at times talking in low, hushed tones. Then the four boys came back again on 22 October and left for Katta the next day, only to be back 15–20 days later, with their bags and roses. This time they came by bus.

"It was harvest time. I finished my household chores hurriedly and rushed off to the fields to help my husband. When I came back, the boys were not in the house. At around 3 or 3.30 p.m., as the sun was slowly losing its ferocity, Salim came to the field. 'Do you need help?' he asked with a smile. I shook my head.

"I noticed Karim had a handkerchief around his palm. He looked frightened. Perhaps he was even trembling. 'What happened?' I asked and touched his bandaged hand lightly.

'Karim needs to be taken to a doctor,' answered Ramesh.

'How did he get injured?'

'He was injured by a scythe while he was trying to cut coconuts from a tree.' Ramesh stared at his toes.

"Karim looked like he was running a temperature. He puked. I gave him lemonade. They left the next day. They came back again, for the third time, on 12 November, carrying a gunny bag filled with roses, and a black plastic sheet. They left for Katta in the morning and returned in the evening. Finally, on the 14th, they left my home about 10 or 10.30 in the morning and returned around 3 p.m. They bathed at the well and left.

"I saw on television that some dead bodies had been found on the hills of Nandos. Four or five days later, the police came down with Ramesh," she concluded.'

'My Lords, now I will read the part regarding her cross examination,' I said. I intended to show them the portions that revealed the weaknesses in her evidence. They had been highlighted carefully.

Justice Gogoi nodded.

I started reading again.

'Is it correct that your husband has been arrested in connection with the murders and you desperately want him to be acquitted?' the defence lawyer—in a bid to break this witness—had asked, and I wanted the judges in the top court to see this.

'It is correct that I strongly feel my husband should be released,' she had replied.

"Do you feel your husband has been wrongly implicated in the case?"

"Yes. Our only mistake was that we allowed the boys to come regularly to our house. My husband was arrested about a week after Ramesh was arrested."

"The boys came to your house and went up to the hillock with guns and rods," the defence lawyer continued. "You never questioned them?"

"No, I never questioned them."

"Is it correct that the police promised you that your husband would be freed if you gave the statement you have given today?"

"No."

"How far is the plateau from your house?"

"I never went to the plateau. I do not know how far it is from my house...There was a single barrel gun in my house. I handed it over to the police after my husband was arrested."'

After reading her evidence aloud, I was ready with my own arguments. As I mentioned earlier, though no fresh evidence is led in the higher courts, it can be re-appreciated. My job was to show that the lower courts had wrongly appreciated the depositions of the witnesses.

'Look at the details she has given before the court, My Lords. Her earlier statement before the police hardly consists of a paragraph! And she has nothing to say against her husband, who was also a co-accused. Please look at what the trial judge has to say about her.' I picked up the volume which contained the judgment rendered by the trial judge. Kamlesh, Mr Gonsalves's assistant, helped me find the correct volume. The court master handed theirs to the judges.

I continued, 'The trial judge says that a witness responds to only those questions which are put to them. It's very surprising then. Maybe no one asked her any question about her husband. My Lords, charges had been framed against her husband,' I said, with one hand on the book from which I was reading, driving the point home, 'but no one asked her a single question about him!'

I could see the judges taking notes. Then I moved on to the next witness: Santosh Yadav.

Santosh Yadav had corroborated the evidence offered by Smita Korgaonkar and confirmed before the court that the boys had visited their house on four or five occasions between October and December 2003. Santosh had been ready to depose against Ramesh. I started reading his examination-in-chief.

'"Ramesh once came to the house wearing a gold chain and a diamond ring. 'Why this change?' his uncle enquired.

'"Ramesh grinned. 'I have started a transport business.'

'"'Hmm…you seem to be doing well.'

'"And then one day Ramesh brought a gun. He kept it in the room where he slept. A cycle tube was wrapped around the barrel of the gun and it came right up to my shoulder. It is the same as Police Article 52 and Court Article P I as was just shown.

'"Ramesh showed me a *ghoda* [revolver], about 10 inches long, with revolving chambers. Yes, yes, I can identify it."'

Santosh Yadav had identified the weapon in the courtroom.

I continued reading what he had said about Ramesh. '"He also carried a grey suitcase and an iron bar, the length of my arm. 'Actually, this is handy for killing fish,' Ramesh had explained when I was examining it."

Santosh Yadav had also identified the iron bar in the courtroom.

room. Karim was holding Ramesh by his collar. He spotted me and let go of the other boy immediately, throwing an apologetic look. 'We had a fight over some money he owed me.'

"I walked away.

"They came to our place again and again. Before leaving, they would pack water, food, some clothes, and the dismantled parts of a gun. Karim had a sword and an iron bar. The sword had a curved iron blade and a wooden handle. It is the same sword you have shown me right now. They always said they were going for hunting and then went up the hills of Nandos. I was surprised to notice that though they wore trousers when they left the house, they came back wearing shorts. They usually carried handbags with chains and belts attached to them.

"When all the boys had gone away, I climbed up to the loft and opened the bundle they had hidden. There were clothes dripping with blood!

"And then one day Karim came to the house, looking terrified. 'Please throw away the dismantled parts of the guns you have here,' he said, looking agitated. Four or five policemen came to our house with Ramesh the next day. And then there was a news report on television that some dead bodies had been found on the plateau of Nandos.'"

I now read the part about Santosh's cross-examination. I feared this witness more than the aunt, Smita. He had described the details so clearly! And he seemed to have no motive to implicate the boys. This boy alone was capable of getting my clients hanged. I was perspiring by the time I finished reading his examination-in-chief. But we lawyers are trained in such a way that our emotions do not show in the courtroom.

I read out everything slowly, revealing absolutely no feelings. We went over the questions asked by the defence lawyer at the trial court.

'"Do you accept that you were treated as the servant of the house and never sent to school?"

'"No. I was treated as a family member," he replied.

'"Then why did you sleep outside while the others slept inside the house? Besides, didn't they leave you to guard the house whenever they had to go out?"

'"Your Honour," the defence lawyer had said, "he was the servant of the house. They did not send him to school; in fact they made him work in the fields, cook, and clean. Yet he has given a false statement because he wants to protect the head of the family. He does not want to lose his job."'

The boy had described the muzzle loader guns, the revolvers, the iron rod, with absolute accuracy.

I continued with the defence lawyer's words:

'"Is it correct that you want Ramesh's uncle to be freed?"

'"Yes."

'"And that you would do anything to get him released?"

'"Yes."

'"Were you told that Ramesh's uncle would be released if you said all this in court?"

'"No. Baba had no role to play in the murders!" he said. "In fact, he asked Ramesh why he had bought three more guns and two revolvers when he already had a licensed gun. Smita *Kaki*, his aunt, did not know about it either."

'"Were the guns broken by Ramesh?"

'"No. They were dismantled. While one gun was divided into three parts, the other was split into four."

'"Was there any identification mark on the parts shown in the courtroom that would confirm that they were parts of the guns possessed by Ramesh?"

'"No."

'"Is it correct that the barrel of the part shown here does not match with the butt of the shortened gun?"

'"Yes. They do not match."'

The cross-examination of Santosh, star witness number two, was complete. He had been believed by the lower courts.

I looked at my watch. It was already 3 p.m. The courts sit till 4 p.m. I wanted to cover at least the star witnesses before it was time for the judges to leave.

I knew many others waited to be heard by the top court. I could not go on and on. So I started reading what the next witness, Sachin Chavan, had to say, a bit hurriedly. Sachin had claimed, during the trial, that he had transported two of the victims to the plateau on his autorickshaw. He had his own story to tell.

'"Ramesh married twice. He looked prosperous and usually visited his uncle once a year, but somehow his visits became more frequent in 2003. Once Karim and Salim came down with two men I did not know. Later on, I learnt their names: Hemant Thakre and Shankar Sarage. I took both men in my rickshaw to the hillock where they were murdered. They seemed to be close friends and they paid their rickshaw fare to me. One was short and fat, with plump cheeks. He held a gunny bag. They had asked me to drive them to Katta. They told me they had come from Mumbai and wanted to meet Babaji—Ramesh Baba. I told them there was no Ramesh Baba. I saw Karim and Salim going towards the plateau with both the men. At that very hour, I saw Ramesh going towards Nandos in his Tata Sumo. I was surprised that those that I carried in my autorickshaw to that place never came back.

'"The police showed me photographs of the two men I had taken in my autorickshaw and wanted me to identify them."

'"And when was this?"' Now I was reading the part where this witness was being cross-examined. Sachin had mentioned all the wrong dates.

'"Did the police beat you?"

'"No. I gave my statement voluntarily. My statement before the judge was recorded at 4 p.m. It is the same statement as is being shown to me right now."

'"Is it correct that you do not have good relations with your brother?"

'"No. It is not correct."

'"Did he invite you when he got married?"

'"No."

'"Why? It shows that you don't have good relations with your brother," the defence lawyer had concluded. "Is that the reason you want him hanged?"

'"No."

'"Did you make any attempt to meet him after he was jailed?"

'"No."

'"Do you realize that your brother can be hanged if the offences are proved against him?"

'"Yes, I know."

'"Did you ever want to meet Ramesh?"

'"No. I did not want to meet him."

'"Did you meet your aunt and her children after that? Did you try to help them?"

'"No."'

I had finished reading the evidence of this witness. There were not many people in the courtroom by now. One of the litigants, a colleague told me later on, had dozed off. He had been asked to leave the courtroom, though I did not blame him. At times, it can be quite monotonous in the courtroom, especially when the proceedings do not concern you.

The brothers of Shyam and Salim also sat at the back. Alert, they hung on to each word I uttered as they tried to gauge the mood of the court. A small wrinkle on the forehead of a judge bothered them, just as a strong point made by me in defence brought some relief.

I had noted the page number where it was recorded in the evidence that Sachin had provided all the wrong dates. I also noted the portion of his evidence where he had accepted that he did not have good relations with his brother, so much so that Ramesh had not even invited him to his wedding.

My job next was to show whether the lower courts had believed this witness. Unlike Santosh, the high court hadn't believed Sachin. It had reached the conclusion that Sachin, a liar, was trying to implicate the boys because he wanted to protect his uncle. I saw the judges note down the page number. Then I did not waste much time on this witness.

The last star witness was Satish Korgaonkar. This witness had tried to prove that Ramesh had used his ill-gotten money, to buy assets such as a Tata Sumo. '"I helped Ramesh in purchasing a Tata Sumo," I read his statement in the courtroom, "though the vehicle was registered in Salim's name."' This witness had also been ready to talk about Ramesh's conduct when the cops came to Suryakant Korgaonkar's house: '"Yes, yes," he had said in his examination-in-chief, "Ramesh hid himself when he heard that the cops had come to his uncle's house. He then pleaded, "Mama, promise to save me if anything happens!"'

I knew there was a clock behind me, and I turned around to see what time it was. I still had 15 minutes, so I continued reading the cross-examination, more confident now after several hours of argument.

'"But you have not stated earlier, before the police, that Ramesh paid Rs 85,000 in the presence of Salim and Karim to buy the car. Also, you stated earlier that Ramesh wanted your car to go to Nandos during the Ganesh festival—one of the occasions when the boys supposedly killed. But this fact is not present in your statement before the police. Don't you think you are improving your statement to help your brother, Suryakant?"'

It was a lacuna in the prosecution's case. I knew it was not very damaging, but I showed it to the top court anyway. I wanted the court to re-appreciate the evidence and be merciful to my boys.

'It is 4.00 o'clock. We will hear this case tomorrow,' said Justice Sathasivam. The ushers in white ran to pull the chairs for the judges.

The judges rose and left.

16

Other Witnesses

I had not revised the portions to be argued yet again. Every time the case reached or was about to reach the desk, I brushed up the main points. I had it all on my fingertips by then. Even now, after so many years, I remember Santosh Yadav was Prosecution Witness No. 75, Smita was No. 4, Dr Jinturkar was No. 76. I also remember whatever they had said before the police and the court.

I did not want to revise the case anymore. I went home, took a quick walk, and went to sleep early. The bags were loaded in the car and we were in the courtroom of the chief justice by 10.15 a.m. the next day. It was a regular day, so there were few lawyers rushing in and out of courtrooms, vying for space. Riyaz had placed all the papers on the table. At exactly 10.30 a.m., the judges entered the courtroom. Instantly, I was on my feet. The judges folded their hands and sat down. My case was   111

OTHER WITNESSES

called out.

I started reading out the statement of Vinod, the boy at Mayur Lodge, who claimed to have seen Salim with the fruit merchant, Kerubhai Mali, and his family. He had said that five persons had come to him on 14 November 2003.

'"Early in the morning at about 7 or 7.30, as I was just about to rise, the bell rang. A middle-aged man, about 40 or 45 years old, wearing a shiny Rado watch on his wrist, stood in front of me. His clothes were white and he carried a grey suitcase measuring 2 ft × 2 ft. There was a woman with him, probably his wife. She was fair and wore a yellow sari. There was a *mangalsutra* around her neck with a Ganesh and Laxmi pendant. Two children stood nearby. A young boy accompanied the family: he was fair, with feline eyes. He was about 25. 'I am Anil Jadhav,' he said, and wrote it down in the register: Anil Jadhav and family. 'The rates are Rs 50 per cot,' I told the woman, and showed them their room. I was the only employee at the lodge at that time.

"The counter of Mayur Lodge is in a room measuring 10 ft × 15 ft, with six chairs. The owner of the lodge sat at the counter. The man in white clothes gave him some money, which he counted and then returned the balance. I changed the bed sheets in their room and fetched four buckets of water for them. Then they went for a walk around 9 a.m. The couple and the young man walked, while the children ran ahead of them. They came back soon, around 11, and left the lodge shortly afterwards.

'"He is the boy who said he was Anil Jadhav," Vinod had said, identifying Salim in the courtroom. Vinod had also identified Kerubhai Mali and his family from the photograph shown to him. Besides that, he had identified the yellow sari worn by his wife, a tattered piece of yellow fabric recovered from the plateau.'

This witness had proved that the Malis were last seen alive in Salim's company. In a case where there is no direct evidence, if the dead victim was last seen alive in the company of the accused, the chances of the accused person's conviction are higher.

I now showed the court how this witness had been cross-examined in the trial court. The defence lawyer had shown a page to Vinod and asked, 'Is it correct that the entries in the register relating to 14 and 15 November 2003 show some erased parts and overwriting?'

Vinod had accepted that the page contained erased parts and overwriting. I showed the page to the court. The prosecution's case was that the Malis were killed on 14 November. Presuming that this boy had seen them on 14 November with Salim, why had the entries been manipulated in the register? Did it not show that the prosecution was overzealous in proving that the case has been solved?

Now I had to present the evidence of the knife maker. I bent down to look for the volume, shuffling some papers. Judicial time is precious; the judges reeled under huge pendency. I could see them growing impatient.

Kamlesh rose, picked up a volume, quickly looked through the index, and handed it over to me with the correct page flagged. I resumed reading.

'"When Karim came to me about a year ago," the ironsmith had stated, "he carried a *patta* [sheet of metal] with him and wanted me to prepare a kitchen knife and a butcher's knife. The kitchen knife I made was 12 inches long and had a wooden handle."

The ironsmith had identified Karim as the boy who came to him with the patta. However, some details of his description of the knives had been wrong.

"But such knives are easily available in the market," he had said.

"Is it correct that you have constructed your hut where you have, without permission?" the defence lawyer had asked.

The ironsmith had denied it.

"He is giving a false deposition," the defence lawyer had argued. "He has motive. He is supporting the police since his hut is an illegal construction in that area and he doesn't want to get into trouble with them."'

The cops had obviously been under immense pressure to solve the case. After all, this case had shaken the state, and the cops wanted to show that they had been quick in nabbing the culprits. The witness had been asked to say whatever they wanted, and he had had no option but to oblige. The chain had to be complete if there was to be a conviction.

The prosecution had produced several witnesses. Some had spoken dispassionately; others had fumbled. Another witness who was important for me was Dr Rane, who claimed to have treated Karim when he had hurt himself. Smita had claimed that she had seen Karim's injury. She had taken him to see Dr Rane. I now wanted to ask the top court to consider whether they should believe him. I wanted the top court to hear what he had said before I offered my own comments.

I resumed reading out from the volumes, pausing to explain only when the judges needed some clarification. After consulting his records, Dr Rane had confirmed that he had treated Karim.

'"Karim came to me around 4.30 p.m.," Dr Rane had said. "He had sustained an injury on the index finger of his right hand. It was an incise wound, about a quarter inch long. I dressed it and gave him an anti-tetanus injection. He appeared frightened and was perspiring profusely when he was brought to me."

'The cross-examination of the doctor went thus:

'"Is it correct that you did not maintain an OPD register?"

'"It is correct that the name of the patient, the date, the treatment given to him, and the fee charged have to be noted in the OPD register. I did not maintain such a register," he had admitted. He could recollect attending to Karim only after consulting his papers. "The injury was muscle deep."

'"Is it correct that in the test identification parade you identified a dummy as Karim?"'

During the test identification parade, the suspect is asked to sit along with a few others. The witness is found to be credible if he recognizes the suspect from among the others. Dr Rane had confessed that he had identified the wrong person during the test identification parade.

'"You couldn't identify Karim in the parade, but you claim to remember distinctly that you treated him? That he was frightened when he came to you? Moreover, Exhibit 185 does not specify the nature of injury suffered," the defence lawyer had concluded his cross-examination with these observations.

Dr Rane was an important witness nonetheless, and I tried to prove that he was not so reliable after all. I read the portion where the doctor had admitted that he could not recognize Karim to the bench once again.

'And what did the trial judge say to that, My Lords?'

By now the trial court judgment was in my hands. I asked the court master to give the judges their copy. 'Dr Rane was the only doctor in the village, and Ramesh's uncle, Suryakant, knew him well. This witness should, therefore, be believed. He may have been the only doctor there, but the question is: was Smita truthful when she said that Karim had injured himself after killing his victims, and that this witness treated him?'

Justice Sathasivam looked at Justice Gogoi, who sat on his right, and Justice Singh, who sat on his left. They discussed something I could not hear. After a while, they looked at me. It was a signal for me to continue.

I had now become bold and argued with ease. The judges were receptive and took notes, interrupting only when they needed clarifications.

The examination of the witnesses had lasted for years. It was very important that I read their statements, especially of those who had provided wrong details or contradicted themselves. A great deal of that had been revealed during the cross-examination. In a criminal case, the guilt has to be proved beyond reasonable doubt, and if I could put enough doubt in the minds of the judges, it would help my case tremendously, even though I knew I was fighting a hopeless case.

Another witness was Hari Patil, a businessman. He was 55. He had identified Karim in the courtroom during the trial. He had claimed that Karim had used his ill-gotten gains to buy a mutton shop from him. The reason I wanted to read out the evidence of this witness was that I wanted to show Justice Sathasivam and his brother judges that payments had been made earlier, even before the boys had allegedly killed. It would thus be wrong to say that the funds for buying the shop came from killing innocent people.

'"I had a mutton shop measuring 8 ft × 9 ft. Karim wanted to purchase it for Rs 2.5 lakh. I received my first payment in cash on 15 June 2003 and then on 25 August. On 1 December the same year, he gave me a cheque of Rs 50,000, which was drawn from Maratha Cooperative Bank. I was scared when he came with the police and I handed over the cash to them."'

The bodies were recovered in 2003, and witnesses were examined for the next six years. There were lengthy cross-examinations and arguments by both the sides. I knew I, too, was taking a lot of time during my arguments in the Supreme Court. Had it not been a death sentence case, the judges would not have heard me for so long. My strategy was to read out the evidence of a witness and then show how the lower courts had dealt with it. I remember the chief justice say, just as I had finished with one witness and turned over pages to show what the next had said, 'This is a good method. You read out the evidence and then show what the trial court and the high court had to say to that.'

Normally, it is the other way round. We discuss the judgments, and then go back to the evidence. I beamed, happy that the chief justice had praised me.

17

SKULLS AND BONES

I knew I was taking more time than the court could afford. Besides the state lawyer who opposed me, Mr Gonsalves, too, needed time to argue on sentencing. But then as Justice Tirath Singh Thakur, the former chief justice of India, who was known for giving a patient hearing to all the lawyers who appeared before him, said in his speech during the retiring chief justice's farewell ceremony, 'It will be most unfair to tell a surgeon to hurry up as others are waiting. Likewise, every litigant comes with a problem and it is the duty of a judge to hear him...The judges become hard-boiled, no doubt, by the time they are elevated to the Supreme Court, but the least we can give a lawyer is a patient hearing.'

The judges in the present case were patient, looking at every scrap of paper of importance with me. But I knew I had to speed up. This was the second day of my argument.

The Supreme Court of India is the last court of appeal. If the special leave petition is dismissed by the judges, a review can be filed against it. Anyone who practises here regularly knows that 99 per cent of review petitions are dismissed. And that leaves you with one last option: a curative petition, which can be filed only after a certificate has been obtained from a designated senior that the case is fit to be filed. And there, too, the dismissal rate is 99.99 per cent!

I knew if at all my clients stood a chance, it was now.

A few lawyers sat in the courtroom. Riyaz stood around for some time and then sat down in a little enclosure at the back. The volumes I needed were on the big table right in front, but what if I needed something else? I could not possibly leave my place and grope around in the bags for that important scrap of paper I needed to show!

I now wanted to prove that the medical experts had not identified the bodies correctly. And until and unless these rotting bodies had been identified, one could not move on to the next step. The dead bodies had been put in plastic sheets after the seals were broken. They lay there like broken toys. The only difference was that no one would have liked to play with these. They were beyond recognition. Modern techniques such as forensics, DNA, and superimposition tests had been adopted to identify them.

I had read with interest how the forensic experts had worked under their chief, Dr Jinturkar. The bodies were kept in a huge room, measuring 20 ft × 15 ft, and the drums for maceration had been placed outside, near the big maceration tank.

Eventually, the bodies were macerated. All the drums had been sealed and left aside for one month. When the bones were clear, they had been sent to the doctors for examination.

The medical experts, too, were important witnesses. They had been cross-examined carefully by the defence lawyer during the trial. Now I showed the judges the part where this particular medical expert had been cross-examined.

'When questioned, the doctor had conceded, "It is correct that it is the duty of the investigating officer to submit information to the doctor conducting the post-mortem; it is also the doctor's responsibility to collect the information from the investigating officer. However, I did not receive information from the police that the bodies had been found in the gaps between the rocks and about 30 feet below the plateau. It is also correct that as the skin and palms were not available in several cases, we were unable to know whether they were defensive postures or reflex actions found in the case of accidental death."

'"The deceased may have died by falling from a high rock," the defence lawyer had argued in the trial court. "These bodies have been recovered from a hillock. Such accidents are not uncommon there."

'The vital organs of soft tissues had not been available, so the cause of death could not be established with certainty. The doctor had said, "Ultrasonic examination can be done to determine whether all the bones belong to the same body or not. This facility is not available in our hospital, so we did not carry out such an examination."

Another hole in the prosecution's case. How can you hang someone from evidence based on such imperfect techniques?

The defence lawyer at the trial court had done his homework well. Once, Ram Jethmalani, the noted criminal lawyer, had told us when we went to brief him about a case, 'A lawyer works like a sage, and while framing questions for cross-examination he thinks of 10 questions and rejects them.'

The defence lawyer had asked if Dr Jinturkar had had prior experience of a group post-mortem. Not so experienced in this area, the doctor may have gone wrong.

'"No," the doctor had said, "I have done it only once before."

'"Can you say with certainty that the injuries found on bodies 1, 4, and 10 have been caused by the weapons shown to you?"

'The doctor had observed the mismatched weapons— parts of the muzzle loader guns that been had been re-aligned in the courtroom—and said, "I cannot say for sure that the injuries on bodies 1, 4, and 10 have been caused by the weapons shown to me."

'"The connection between the wounds and the recovered weapons cannot be established," the defence lawyer had thus proved.'

I paused here, hoping the judges would realize that just because the cops had claimed a few guns were recovered from the boys did not prove that those guns had been used to kill.

Santosh, the boy who lived at Suryakant's house and who had claimed to have enough evidence against the boys, had been quite compelling in the courtroom with his descriptions. He had said that the accused had carried iron bars with them. I read out what the forensic expert had had to say about that.

'"In case of a blow by the iron bar, an examination of the brain matter would help in determining the cause of death," the doctor had said. "And no brain matter was available to verify such an injury in this case."

'Just two more witnesses, My Lords,' I raised two of my fingers in a V, pleading for time. The judges nodded. Quickly, I turned the pages to show the evidence of Ratnaprabha Gujarathi, the superimposition expert. She had been required to confirm whether the skulls shown to her belonged to the people in the photographs. In the witness box in the lower court she had given a brief outline of her work, and the job she did. In her examination–in-chief, she stated that after conducting the tests, she had concluded that the skulls in exhibits 1, 3, and 5 could have belonged to the victims in exhibits 2, 4, and 6 respectively. 'They *could* have belonged?' the defence lawyer had asked. 'Is your report based on conjectures?'

I now started reading out Ratnaprabha's cross-examination—the portion marked carefully with a pink highlighter I had picked up from my daughter's pencil box.

'"Is it correct that the mandibles—the lower jaw bones—of all the three skulls were missing? How can you give a correct report when parts of the skull were missing?"

'"I asked the police to supply the missing mandibles but I was told that they were not available."

'"Ms Ratnaprabha, how can you say with such confidence that the skulls examined by you belong to the people in the photograph?"

'"I rely on Modi and Parekh for my tests," she had said, drawing support from two authoritative books on medical jurisprudence and toxicology. "My conclusions are 99 per cent correct."'

The defence lawyer had done his research well. He went through the chapter on superimposition as discussed in the books, and passed on the volume to this important witness in the courtroom. Every word uttered by her brought my clients closer to the gallows. Granted, the boys had confessed they had killed, but torture can compel anyone to confess to a crime—even if it was not committed by them. And whom had they killed? This woman seemed to have come up with an answer. But was it the right answer—without an iota of doubt?

The witness was shown the relevant portions in the book, which had been marked, probably by a junior who had worked with the defence lawyer on the brief. It said the science of superimposition was imperfect.

'Superimposition tests are more or less guesswork,' I told the judges in the Supreme Court. While drafting my own petition, I had quoted from books by Modi and Parekh and carried them with me to the courtroom. I showed the pages supporting my argument.

'My Lords, the cops picked up a few skulls, beat the poor boys to pulp, and made them write a confession. But whose skulls are these? Such methods do not always give accurate results. These may not be the skulls of the people in the photographs at all. Will My Lords hang the boys on the basis of this kind of evidence?'

The judge noted down something. The examination of the superimposition expert was over.

'One last witness,' I said, 'and I will conclude my arguments.' I was referring to Dr S. Pandurang, the DNA expert. DNA results give information about genealogy or ancestry.

'The doctor's office had acknowledged the receipt of samples sent by the Malwan Police Station through the superintendent of police, Sindhudurg. He had received 10 bone samples and 15 blood samples. The blood samples had been received from the family members of those believed to be dead. The bones of the dead and the blood samples of their supposed relatives were matched to see if they were really related. The diary recovered from the hillock had telephone numbers of some of the relatives and friends of the dead. Those whose names were mentioned in the diary had been contacted, and if someone happened to be a relative of the person suspected killed, their blood sample and the bone sample of the deceased were matched by the DNA expert to find out whether the two were related.

'Dr Pandurang had noted that out of the 10 bones sent, only four—those of bodies 1, 6, 8, and 10 were suitable for DNA analysis. He had written to the superintendent of police immediately. "Can you send any other body part of bodies 2, 3, 4, 5, 7, and 9?"

'In response, six femur bones had been sent to him. The bones of bodies 2 and 7 were found to be in acceptable condition for DNA analysis. Dr Pandurang had then set out to compare the bone samples with the DNA profiles of the blood samples. Conclusions were drawn based on the DNA analysis. However, as some blood samples were not fit for use, the results would be incorrect. The doctor had signed his name at the foot of every page of the report. The outer box, which contained the remains, was sealed. It bore the seal of Centre for DNA Fingerprinting and Diagnostics (CDFD). The remains of the samples had been brought to the court with the help of the police.'

After reading out these details in haste, I leapt to the part where the cross examination of this witness was recorded, slightly relieved that I was about to conclude my arguments. This case had been taking up all my time. I would relax after this and concentrate on other cases.

'"Were the blood samples not contaminated?" the defence lawyer had asked the witness. "Were the samples fit for examination when you set out to do your work?"

'Dr Pandurang had admitted that the samples may have been contaminated, for they were examined very late—and this may have led to incorrect conclusions.'

DNA science is not very developed in India. Kits used for examination are usually imported from the US, where there are Acts regulating their use. The cross-examination went on.

'"Is it correct that in India no Central or State Act has been enacted regulating DNA analysis?"

'"Yes."

'"Is it correct that there is no control to audit and supervise the work done by the officials of CDFD?"

'Dr Pandurang had answered in the affirmative.

'That's it, My Lords,' I bowed slightly, closing the volume in my hand. It was a huge relief that I was finally done. It was Mr Gonsalves's turn now.

18

THE FINAL LAP I

A heavy curtain hung on the main door of the court. The national emblem, Asiatic lions standing back to back, could be seen at the centre, just above the judges' heads, with *yato dharmastato jaya*—dharma leads to victory—written below.

Earlier, the courtroom had been carpeted. Now, we have a bare wooden floor. It is easier to clean. There were boards on either side of the room showing case status; lawyers could keep tabs on cases going on in other courtrooms.

Thick, bound volumes of Supreme Court cases containing important judgments passed previously, stood in rows on the shelves. When such an instance was cited by a lawyer, the librarian handed over the relevant book to the judges.

Mr Gonsalves now stood before the judges and placed his papers on the lectern. He had brought photocopies of the book, *Resheemganth* (*The Silken Knot*) written and translated by our young clients in the jail.

'Court Master, please hand these over to My Lords,' he said, picking up the volumes. The court master was a young lady in a silk sari and a black coat. She obliged.

'My Lords have held earlier that a convict should be hanged only when he or she is a threat to society. These young boys are full of life. How can they be a threat to anyone? Please do read the book written by them.'

Justice Sathasivam smiled. 'Where is the time?'

Many judges, including the former chief justice, Justice Dattu, have admitted that they read 15 or 16 hours every day. They, too, read the cases before they come to the courtroom, just as we lawyers do.

'The boys have been in jail for more than 10 years,' Mr Gonsalves stepped forward, 'and there has not been a single incident to show that they are demonic or unfit to live in civilized society.'

I sat beside him, relaxed now that my role was over. I knew that the high court judges had been acquainted with these facts, yet they had shown no mercy. It was with some misgiving that I listened to him.

'And what have the boys been doing in jail all this while?' He pulled out his notes, which revealed that the boys had educated themselves in prison. We had made a chart in his office in which we had tabulated the qualifications of each. 'All of them are graduates now and, more importantly, they have done courses in Gandhian thought.'

He then put the judgment of the Mumbai bomb blast case forward, and argued that if anyone should be hanged, it was Ramesh; the others should be spared.

I flinched with shock. Ramesh was *my* client. I was his advocate on record! And then my senior continued in the same breath, 'Why should *any*one be hanged, for that matter? The high court judges saw the faces of the accused and to them they appeared beyond reform. It is incorrect. Maybe the boys were acting brave and hiding their true feelings. Who would not be scared at the thought of death?'

He cited some foreign judgments, cases similar to this one, where the courts had refused to award death penalty to the accused.

It was lunch time. The judges left. They would be back by 2 p.m.

'Go, get these judgments,' Mr Gonsalves instructed Kamlesh. Kamlesh wrote down the citations on a small piece of paper and was back within 15 minutes, loaded with other thick volumes of Supreme Court cases.

We did not go for lunch. I, too, showed a judgment to my senior, rendered by Justice Sathasivam. It was the case of a man called Mulla. The chief justice had observed that an important mitigating factor *Bachan Singh*[1,2] had missed was the socio-economic one. A poor man stands a better chance of reformation and should not be hanged. The boys were poor, I had emphasized while drafting the case, quoting extensively from *Mulla*.[3]

The judges were back in the courtroom promptly at 2 p.m. 'The wind seems to be blowing in your favour,' the chief justice had told Mr Gonsalves, who was now on his feet, 'though we can say nothing right now.' They must have discussed the case in their chamber or in the corridor at the back.

I have gone that side on a few occasions—the judges' side. These keepers of peace have to lead secluded lives and not mingle with lawyers and the common public, probably to avoid their judgments being influenced. When I went that side for the first time with an appointment, I saw a long, heavily carpeted corridor, with chambers of judges on both sides. There were more chambers on the next floor, connected to this level by a short flight of stairs. Maybe the judges assembled in this very corridor every day before they proceeded towards the courtrooms. Maybe it was here that they had discussed my case for a few minutes, just before they re-entered the courtroom.

Mr Gonsalves took 10 more minutes.

Then the chief justice turned to the state lawyer. 'You have two hours,' he said. 'Show us the portions that endorse your arguments.'

Notes

1. Bachan Singh vs State of Punjab (1979) 3 SCC 727.
2. Bachan Singh vs State of Punjab (1980) 2 SCC 684.
3. Mulla and Another vs State of U.P. (2010) 3 SCC 508.

19

THE FINAL LAP II

Mr Gonsalves had left the courtroom after making his submissions. I took his place. I listened to the counter arguments carefully so that I could offer rejoinders if needed. It felt like a passenger on a train about to reach its destination. Other lawyers waited like co-passengers, hoping their case would be heard soon.

The special public prosecutor who had argued the case in the trial court was also present. He was a middle-aged man and wore a red *tika* on his forehead. The panel lawyer for the state of Maharashtra in the Supreme Court, Sushil Karanjakar, a thin man with a short beard, argued the case on its behalf. He was from Satara, Maharashtra. Though he had started his practice from the Bombay High Court, he had finally shifted to the Supreme Court in 1996–97. He read the high court judgment and repeated how gruesome the murders had been.

The state lawyer showed paragraph 96 of the high court judgment where the circumstances held to be proved were set out. The killings were brutal, he said. The boys had been barbarous, refusing to spare innocent children and a woman. If someone had not made the anonymous call to the police station, they would have killed more people.

The prosecution had worked hard, using all the modern techniques to identify the bodies that had been mutilated, apparently to destroy evidence.

The chain was complete, he argued further, and repeated the gory details. The case was the result of meticulous planning and it was but natural that there would be no eyewitnesses. However, one incriminating circumstance after another proved the boys to be guilty. The prosecution had proved its evidence beyond reasonable doubt.

'These demons are a threat to the society, My Lords,' he concluded, 'and if let off, they will kill more innocents.' He closed the volume that contained the high court judgment.

The order was reserved. The lawyers on both sides were permitted to file written submissions, if any, within a week.

20

THE JUDGMENT

It was late in the evening on 26 February 2014 when Riyaz said to me, 'Ma'am, your death sentence matter is listed for pronouncement of judgment tomorrow.' The daily cause list had been uploaded on the Supreme Court website. The final list is generally uploaded in the evening, when it starts getting dark and the streets are bathed in lights. Riyaz sat making a list of cases on his laptop, with his head bowed, double-checking so as to avoid missing out on any case. Next, he gave the print command. The paper rolled off the printer, and I held it up. The case was on the top of the board in court no. 1, where the chief justice sat.

Oh God, so the judgment was about to be declared! I felt like a schoolgirl who, after having toiled day and night, was waiting to see if all the hard work had paid off. I dialled my senior's number, half suspecting he wouldn't take it; seniors are generally busy holding conferences during this time as they prepare for the next day. Mr Gonsalves answered my call immediately. I gave him the news.

'I am scared,' he said.

'So am I, sir!' I replied.

Salim's mother called me up late at night. Maybe she had taken my number from my senior's office. I had not met her, though Salim's brother had been attending court. I tried to imagine myself in her place. If I, as a lawyer, felt so shaky, she must have been going through hell. We spoke about Salim for a while.

'I want to come to the court tomorrow. How do I do it on such short notice?' she asked.

'You need not come. I will tell you what the court has held.'

'No ma'am, I will come.' Her voice was firm.

'All right. Let me see what I can do...'

Later, I told Riyaz as he picked up his helmet, ready to exit the office, 'We will have to leave for the court a little early tomorrow. Getting the passes made will take some time.'

The usual time we—my husband Braj, Riyaz, and I—leave for the court is around 9 a.m.

'Please ask her not to come,' Riyaz had pleaded with a worried look on his face. 'She will faint in the courtroom.' My clerk had been closely associated with the case and even he knew we did not stand much of a chance. For months, Ballu and Riyaz had carried those three heavy bags to the court on almost all regular days while we waited for the case to be heard. This was in addition to the papers they had carried for other cases.

I shook my head. 'I told her, but she refused to stay back.'

At 9 a.m., I received another call from the woman.

'We are at the Supreme Court, where they issue gate passes,' she said. 'We need your signature to enter, ma'am.' A litigant can enter the courtroom only if a senior lawyer or her advocate on record has signed the application for an entry pass. Along with the signature, a seal or a stamp has to be affixed. Passes are issued on a first-come-first-serve basis, subject to the availability of seats. The court and item numbers have to be mentioned clearly.

The security was not as tight in the top court two decades ago, when I started my practice. Lawyers and litigants could easily enter the courtrooms, outside which stood an armed cop. It is not so now. After the bomb blast at the Delhi High Court, and persistent threats, the top court has been converted into some sort of a fortress with layers of security.

Ballu drove fast, at times overspeeding. We took the DND, the expressway connecting Delhi to Noida, with no pedestrian crossings or intersections. This helps in driving fast and safely. We zoomed past the other cars in silence. I looked out of the window; everyone seemed to be in a hurry. I glanced at my watch every now and then. Finally, we were in the court premises by 10.15 a.m.

'The pronouncement is at 10.30,' I told Riyaz, hurrying towards court no. 1. 'Go, get their passes made quickly.'

Inside the courtroom, I was right at the front with Mr Gonsalves. The counsel for the state of Maharashtra was also present. The room was packed. A colleague smiled at me. We often had coffee together. I offered her a feeble smile in return. The litigants and their relatives sat at the back in the enclosure. I wondered if the mothers of my clients could make it to the courtroom in time.

The judges assembled exactly at 10.30 a.m., just as the ushers ran to pull their chairs back. Folding their hands, they took their seats. In spite of the crowd, there was complete silence. Justice Gogoi had written the judgment on behalf of the bench. It was dated 27 February 2014. We hung on to each word he read out from the operative portion. Once or twice he glanced at me. The tension probably showed on my face. The other judges sat calmly, staring in front.

The court held that the boys were *not to be hanged*.

'Thank God!' I cried, and was slightly ashamed when I realized my voice had carried in the courtroom. Somehow it sounded immature to my own ears. Lawyers are not supposed to show such emotion at work. 'Yes, thank God,' my senior echoed. I felt better. So he was as emotional about this case as I was.

I wanted to savour this moment, enjoy it like a child who eats a favourite chocolate bit by bit, not wanting to finish it too soon. I don't know how those boys looked, having never met them, but I could already imagine their smiling, triumphant faces.

I turned around and saw the mothers of Salim and Karim sitting at the back. Oh, the courtroom was so crowded! Lawyers stood in the aisle, jostling for space. Had the women heard the judge? Had Justice Gogoi been loud enough to be audible at the back? I did not know. I could see the mothers leaning against the horizontal bars, straining their ears to learn what was going on.

After the judges had signed at the end, the next case was called out. I bowed slightly and left the courtroom.

Karim and Salim's brothers were out in the corridor, near a big pillar where we had often stood. But this time their mothers were with them. I met Salim's mother for the first time. She was shorter and spoke in a typical Marathi accent. She talked a lot. Karim's mother, on the other hand, spoke little. Salim's mother smiled. Of course she would! The top court had shown mercy to her son!

So these were the women whose sons had been called 'monsters'. What a horrible feeling! But at that moment they hardly cared about the past. They wanted to hear, again and again, what Justice Gogoi had just read out. We still stood near the flight of steps in front of the chief justice's court, where there were tiny pots with blooming flowers. The women chattered nonstop. Shyam's mother was dead, but his brother stood there, beaming, his eyes moist. No one from Ramesh's family was present, but I am sure the news must have made his mother happy.

Once I was back in office I read the entire judgment. It was long. The court had noted my contention that in the absence of any direct evidence, the prosecution had to prove not only that all incriminating circumstances had been laid before the court, but also that there was no room for doubt that it was the boys alone who had committed the crime.

Justice Gogoi had written that I had presented parts of the evidence of important witnesses that contained ambiguities and embellishments. The court noted my argument that the identity of the bodies recovered was doubtful, as they were extremely decomposed; the DNA mapping and the superimposition tests results were inconclusive. Also, some of the registers in the lodges and hotels where the victims had supposedly stayed contained overwriting, additions, and deletions.

The arguments of the state counsel had been noted too. The absence of eyewitnesses or direct evidence, he had said, was natural, as the killings had been planned meticulously. The prosecution had managed to establish highly incriminating circumstances beyond doubt, which showed that the accused were the ones who had killed. The contents of paragraph 96 of the high court judgment were also mentioned. The substratum of the evidence had then been analysed.

The court was of the view that there was no doubt that the deaths were homicidal and the identities of the bodies stood established.

When all this was pieced together, the inescapable conclusion was that my clients had killed.

The court went on to discuss the death penalty jurisprudence. Yes, the debate was on. Cases such as *Jagmohan*[1] and *Bachan Singh*[2,3] the landmark judgments where the top court had debated and laid down the law about whether a convict was to be hanged or spared, were discussed. Justice Gogoi had then wondered: was the option of life sentence available to the boys?

I scrolled the pages hurriedly on my laptop. The murders were brutal, the judges knew. However, the evidence was circumstantial in nature, the boys were poor, and had been on death row for a long period. These were the mitigating factors. And the state had not been able to show that the accused were beyond reform. The court believed in reformation and rehabilitation and opposed the idea of retribution.

I nodded in approval.

The relatives of the boys—basically their brothers—got in touch with me again.

'How do we access the judgment?' they asked.

'Go to the website of Supreme Court,' I told them. 'The judgment has been uploaded.'

By now I was hungry. Pulling open my refrigerator, I took out some peanut butter. As I spread a thick layer on a slice of bread, my thoughts went back to the boys.

I continued reading, munching on the snack. The boys were not bloodthirsty hounds, eager to create further trouble if left loose. They had matured over the years, learnt new things, developed new perspectives, and written a book. The court had, therefore, commuted the sentence of death to life imprisonment in its concluding paragraph.

I turned off the laptop, and started reading another brief—preparation for the next day. I picked up a pencil and started underlining the pertinent portions, scribbling on the page attached for making notes.

Notes

1. Jagmohan Singh vs State of U.P. (1973) 1 SCC 20.
2. Bachan Singh vs State of Punjab (1979) 3 SCC 727.
3. Bachan Singh vs State of Punjab (1980) 2 SCC 684.

21

AFTERWARDS

———

As a child, I always thought those who were arrested for a crime were dangerous—to be kept in jails, like ferocious animals in cages. As I grew older I realized that just about anyone could turn into a criminal. It could be me, my siblings, or our children. One wrong step taken in the heat of passion or while dreaming of riches, and everything is over. You lose freedom for your entire life, you may even get death—as in the case of my boys.

I had worked hard to defend them. They were poor boys, just past adolescence, and had been locked up on death row in Nagpur Jail near the gallows. Had the death sentence been confirmed, how would have they reacted? Would they have slept the night before finally being hanged?

They had evolved enough in the jail, and their learning must have helped them cope with the pressure they were under, diverting their minds from the noose that must have featured in their nightmares day and night. Thank god they were spared. Several others have not been so fortunate.

I don't pretend to be some sort of a messiah for the poor, though many of my clients are underprivileged. Neither am I one. I simply do my duty as a lawyer. While in college, I tried to join the Students Federation of India, a party with Marxist leanings, but with poor marks in the first year of graduation, my enthusiasm for politics soon evaporated.

That is how it begins. Just open the newspaper in the morning. The pages are full of stories of crime, not because crime titillates, but because crimes take place every day, every minute. At this very moment, perhaps a husband is killing his wife, enraged that she did not give him food on time! The reasons are as stupid as this. And after that, scared that he may be caught and sent to the gallows, he will chop her body into small pieces and then spend his entire life dodging the police and the courts.

I am not writing this book to pass judgments. Many will surely pounce on me and argue how harrowing it is for the victim and her/his family. 'Why don't you place yourself in the position of the mother of the victim?' many will say. 'You will feel the pain if your own child is killed!'

A few years ago when brave Jyoti Singh Pandey, the aspiring paramedic, was brutally killed, this was the stand all my friends took. They were my schoolmates, and were shocked to know that I sympathized with those 'despicable characters'.

'I, too, have a daughter who has just turned 16,' I had said. 'It isn't true that I am not sensitive towards the victim or women in general. All I am saying is that we are not gods. At times we may be wrong. Sometimes we turn out to be mistaken even when all the evidence is pointing in a certain direction. So it is not right to jump to conclusions.'

Petitions challenging life imprisonment are dismissed in a routine manner by the top court every day. I have handled many such cases; not one stirred my emotion the way this case did. Someone had killed his wife and hidden her body in a septic tank. Another had struck a fellow guard with a knife 21 times for teasing a woman. In another case, a woman, along with her paramour, had killed her husband and hidden his body under the wooden floor. Then there was a boy who had allegedly raped a woman and burnt her.

Most of them had been in jail for at least seven or eight years when the case reached the top court. A few more years, and they would be free. Some were even acquitted, like the boy who supposedly raped and burnt a woman. It sounds gross and many might disapprove of the fact that I defended him as a lawyer, but a lawyer or a judge cannot pass judgments on the basis of emotion or public hysteria; they have to study the *evidence*.

An accused is presumed innocent unless proved guilty. Even if a dying woman gives a statement, but her versions of the incident differ (in one report she was raped and killed, while in another the stove had burst while she was cooking), it is but natural for the courts to give the benefit of doubt to the accused.

Coming back to the boys, the media had covered their case widely—calling them devils and demons. Anyone who read those news reports would certainly have felt that the boys deserved to die. But those in the media had not read the actual evidence that we lawyers and judges had. And many cases that seem straightforward and revolting

on the surface are found to be perfect frame-ups in reality.
At times the truth emerges long after the wrong person has
been arrested and hanged.

Doctors and lawyers are professionals; they do their
work in a dispassionate way, with little or no emotion.
They are not supposed to be sentimental. They deal with
a case and move on. And this had been my attitude while
fighting various cases—civil, criminal, or constitutional.
But not this time. This case was different. It taught me to
feel and believe in what I was fighting for, and I realized
that there was nothing wrong with it. Though I try giving
my 100 per cent to all the cases I take up, for this case I had
toiled much more than usual. After all, four lives hung in
the balance—and quite literally!

I am happy that all my hard work paid off. It was
pleasing to hear from Salim's mother after the judgment of
commutation was passed by the Supreme Court, 'Ma'am,
the children have to come home. Can we get a certified
copy of the judgment?'

Perhaps they were up for parole.

I was happy.

22

THE ABOLITION OF THE DEATH PENALTY: GLOBAL PERSPECTIVES

The world over, there was a time when a convict was hanged in full public view for murder. His (or her) limp body would dangle mid-air. Children would poke at it sometimes when they passed it, simply out of curiosity. Things changed gradually, and resistance to such kinds of punishment grew. More and more people wanted such an inhuman practice to be done away with. One by one, all European countries abolished the death penalty, as they realized that hanging a convict served no real purpose; it was barbaric and needed to end. Now more than 140 nations worldwide have discarded capital punishment.[1]

In the Middle East, however, we still see primitive methods of hanging. The convict is dragged to the platform, wailing and resisting, and hanged in front of a large crowd. At times, they are brought with hands bound behind them. The executioner forces them to kneel on the ground and slices off their neck with a powerful blow. The prisoner's body turns limp and the head rolls off on the ground. The executioner then wipes off the blood from the headless torso just as a butcher would do.

The US abolished the death penalty in the 1970s, only to reinstate it later through a judgment of the supreme court. The subject is still being debated all over the country. Many want it to be abolished again. Many states have, in fact, abolished it. The reasons, they say, are obvious: it is normally the poor who get the lethal injection. They are victims of inadequate or ineffective legal representation. At times, the execution may be botched. It happened to a prisoner from the state of Oklahoma, Clayton Lockett.[2] Born in 1975 to a drug addict mother and abandoned by her at the age of three, he was raised by his father, who abused him throughout his childhood. Given drugs at a young age, Lockett was taught to steal and never get caught.

Lockett was on death row for shooting 19-year-old high school graduate Stephanie Neman, a witness to his crimes. He had shot her with a sawed off shotgun and watched as she was buried alive by his two accomplices. This took place in 1999. Given the way he had killed the girl, some people felt he should die likewise—in as much pain as his victim had suffered. On 29 April 2014, the day chosen to kill him, he was seen twisting and turning, unable to speak, from the effects of the poison injected into his body. He struggled violently.

Lockett died of a heart attack a little later.

The way he was treated was inhuman. There was public outcry and a fresh debate began on whether the death penalty should be given at all. Here is yet another account of an execution in the American state of Arizona, of Don Harding, who got the gas chamber in 1992.[3] 'His face was red and contorted as if he was attempting to fight through tremendous pain ... Don's body started convulsing violently ... the veins in his temple and neck began to bulge until I thought they might explode ... After several more minutes, the most violent of the convulsions subsided. At this time the muscles around Don's left arm and back began twitching in a wave-like motion under his skin. Spittle drooled from his mouth ... Don Harding took 10 minutes and 31 seconds to die.'

If you cannot give convicts a painless death, don't kill them! In India, the executioner is supposed to break the criminal's neck with the jerk of the rope, but often this is not done properly. The convict is hanged, but if he doesn't die the first time, the hangman repeats the process. To my mind, nothing can be crueller.

There is also another aspect—that of ethnicity. In the US, more African Americans are on death row than Whites, and their execution far outnumbers that of other races. The races of the victim and the accused in capital punishment cases are major factors in determining who is sentenced to die.

In 1990, a report from US Accounting office concluded that studies revealed that the race of the victim was found to influence the likelihood of being charged with capital murder or receiving the death penalty, that is, those who murdered Whites were more likely to be sentenced to death than those who murdered African Americans.[4]

There are far greater chances of conviction if the offender is an African American before an all-White jury, especially when the victim is White. Although almost half of those murdered in the US are African Americans, 77 per cent of those executed, since 1977, were found guilty of murdering White victims. When the colour of skin decides whether one will die or not, it is high time the justice system should ask the question: should death be given at all, especially by a select few who may be prejudiced against the accused for various reasons?

In India, too, the class bias is obvious. And there are hard facts to prove this. A study was conducted by National Law University students, with the help of the Law Commission, and they came up with definite proof that the poor and those belonging to the backward classes get the gallows, while the rich escape. The wealthy and the privileged can afford to engage a battery of lawyers well versed with the law and ready to burn the midnight oil to find loopholes in the prosecution's case. Most of the others cannot. National Law University students interviewed 373 death row convicts over a 15-year period and found that 75 per cent of those given the death penalty belonged to backward classes, religious minorities, and were from economically weaker sections. As many as 93.5 per cent of those sentenced to death for terror offences were Dalits or religious minorities. The gallows are thus only for the marginalized.[5] This, to my mind, is definitely not 'equality before the law and equal protection of law'—a fundamental right granted by the Constitution, which is the holy book for our lawmakers and protectors of civil society.

An argument generally offered in favour of the death penalty is that it seeks to make an example of the person on death row and bring about deterrence. No one will ever dare to kill a fellow being or commit a heinous crime after seeing the horrifying manner in which a brutal criminal is executed.

But the question is: does execution really bring about deterrence? There aren't too many statistics available to support this view, either in India or abroad. There is also little evidence to prove that the countries that have abolished the death penalty have a greater incidence of crime than those that have retained it.

Let us take the case of an innocent man on death row. The judicial system not only in India but the world over is imperfect. To nail an accused, one tends to rely on eyewitnesses, the circumstances, and various reports given by the experts: forensic, DNA, etc. Eyewitness accounts and the depositions of other witnesses may be full of discrepancies, showing that the witness lied or that his/her report is not foolproof. This can be brought out by a good lawyer during cross-examination. The flaws are revealed to the judge at the time of the final arguments when the question of conviction and the sentence are decided. But what if the lawyer fails or is incompetent?

Consider this: a defence lawyer who has not been paid much may participate in the trial in a half-hearted manner and not work hard enough to discover and point out flaws in the prosecution's case. Lawyers have to earn to keep their office running. A meagre fee is hardly an incentive to work hard. A rich client thus stands a better chance of winning their case, while their poor counterpart is left to rot in jail, and, at times, face the hangman's noose.

Beside several other factors, the size of one's pocket, skin colour, political strength, or affiliation can decide whether one should be hanged or not. Is that justice?

Kanimozhi, a member of the Indian parliament, highlighted these factors in her article published in the *Hindu* on 5 June 2013.[6] She wrote, 'On 3 June 1949, Professor Shibbanlal Saxena, a freedom fighter who had been on death row for his involvement in the Quit India Movement, spoke in the Constituent Assembly of how he had seen innocent people being hanged for murder during his days in prison. Proposing the abolition of the death penalty, he said that the avenue of appealing to the Supreme Court "will be open to people who are wealthy, who can move heaven and earth but the common people who have no money and who are poor will not be able to avail themselves of it".'

Kanimozhi said in the same piece, 'Last year, 14 eminent retired judges wrote to the President, pointing out that the Supreme Court had erroneously given death penalty to 15 people since 1996, of whom two were hanged. The judges called this "the gravest common miscarriage of justice in the history of crime and punishment in independent India".

They were talking about the wrongful execution of Ravji Rao and Surja Ram. It is chilling to read about the execution of a person who did not deserve to die. Ravji Rao Ramchandra was a tribal who lived in Rajasthan's Banswara district. He was convicted and later sentenced to death for killing his pregnant wife and three young children. There was no apparent reason for the gruesome killings. Why did the man suddenly kill his wife and children while they were sleeping? No one had an answer. He was also convicted for the attempted murder of his mother and a neighbour's wife, and for killing another man, Gulabji, who was coming towards the house of the neighbour when he heard her shrieks.

Ravji was sentenced to death on 5 December 1994. This was confirmed by the top court in 1996, which held that 'it is the nature and gravity of the crime and not the criminal, which are germane for consideration of appropriate punishment in a criminal trial'.[7] He was hanged in May 1996 at Central Jail in Jaipur. As he approached the gallows, he asked for forgiveness, to which Mr Bissa, the jail superintendent, replied, 'You forgive us.'

The 14 retired judges acknowledged that Ravji was wrongfully executed, his punishment based on an incorrect reading of *Bachan Singh*'s ruling. He was sentenced to death for the crime committed, and important circumstances, such as the socio-economic factors responsible for his action, were not considered at the stage of sentencing. This was a flawed understanding of the law as laid down by the top court in *Bachan Singh*, the judges said.

Similarly, Surja Ram, a poor agriculturist, lived with his two brothers, Dalip Ram and Raji Ram, near Gorakhpur in Uttar Pradesh. They stayed together, though their parents had divided the property: 13 *killas* each to him and his brother, Dalip Ram, and 14 *killas* to Raji Ram. Surja Ram wanted to erect a wire fencing, to which Raji Ram objected. On 7 August 1990, at about 9 p.m., Raji's family went to sleep after dinner. Dalip Ram and his wife were asleep in the inner courtyard, while Raji and his two sons—Naresh and Ramesh—slept in their outer room. Raji's wife, Phoola Devi, daughter Sudesh, and his sister, Niko Bai slept in the courtyard. Surja's wife, Imarti, was asleep in her courtyard.

About 12.30 a.m., Dalip Ram woke up suddenly hearing Sudesh's cries. He saw his brother, Surja, strike Sudesh with a *kassi*, a small spade. Sudesh was severely injured on the neck. Surja escaped even as they tried to get him. Niko was found dead, while Phoola was gasping for breath. Dalip rushed inside the room, only to find Raji Ram and Naresh dead. Ramesh, though alive at that time, was critically injured. He died a little later. Sudesh and Phoola were taken in a vehicle to a hospital at Singharia. Both survived.

The courts refused to show mercy towards the killer. The top court ordered on 25 September 1996 that Surja Ram be hanged, yet again ignoring the law laid down in *Bachan Singh*.[8] On 6 April 1997, the convict was executed.

I remember the public uproar that followed the rape and murder of the aspiring paramedic, Jyoti Singh Pandey, in Delhi. Jyoti was born and raised in Delhi though her parents came from a small village in Ballia district of Uttar Pradesh. On 16 December 2012, the young girl boarded a bus in Munirka, a neighbourhood in South Delhi. It was late in the evening. She had gone to watch a movie with her friend, Awindra Pratap Pandey, a software engineer from Gorakhpur. To get back home, the two friends caught a bus.

Inside were six men, including Ram Singh, the driver, and his brother, Mukesh Singh. Both lived in the cramped Ravidas Camp, a slum in South Delhi. The others included Vinay Sharma, an assistant gym instructor, and Pawan Gupta, who sold fruit for a living. The other two were Akshay Thakur, who had come to Delhi seeking employment, and a 17-year-old juvenile from Badaun.

The six men dragged Jyoti to the rear of the bus, beat her with a rod, and raped her while the driver continued to drive. Medical reports indicated that a rod had been shoved into her vagina, which, as described by the cops later on, was a rusted L-shaped object—something like a wheel jack handle. After they were done, they threw her body out of the moving bus. The youngest of them had allegedly been the most brutal. The viciousness with which she and her friend—who was beaten up brutally—were treated will give anyone shivers.

The victim was found by a passer-by around 11 p.m. He called the Delhi police. Jyoti Singh Pandey was taken to Safdarjung Hospital along with her friend, where she was put on a mechanical ventilator. After battling for her life for a while, the girl died. Her words, as she was dying, still echo in our minds, 'Mother, I want to live.'

It was certainly a gruesome incident and stayed in the national newspaper headlines for several days. On social networking sites, everyone was horrified. Everyone wanted death for the men/boys accused of killing her.

I differed, but hardly any of my friends seemed to agree with me. 'Then how do you create deterrence?' asked one of my friends, Gyanlata.

'Will hanging the accused really lead to fewer rapes in the country?' I asked her.

Other friends of mine quite literally pounced on me for not wanting the perpetrators hanged.

'Will it give pleasure to Jyoti's mother?' I went on. 'Will she revel at the sight of these men hanging by their neck, while their mothers wait outside the gate to receive their dead bodies?'

A dead body is heavy, especially when it happens to be your child. The family of the convict on death row loses everything: land, money, security—all for no fault of theirs. For years, they run from pillar to post and try to engage lawyers—usually an expensive task—in a desperate attempt to save their errant child. Some sell their property and everything they own—even the shirt on their back.

Cases of rape are not uncommon in Delhi even now. Whether the majority agrees with me or not, the fact is that hanging one or two rapists is not a solution, no matter how furious we may be. Newspapers are still full of reports of crimes against women every day. What we need is to study the socio-economic reasons leading to these crimes and bring about changes accordingly. It is the cause that needs to be addressed, not the effect. All the four accused in Jyoti's case were poor men, with little or no education. If, for a minute, we focus not on what they did but what made them do it, perhaps we'll be able to see that the crime may have been committed as an outlet for the frustration they felt towards society. Maybe the men thought this was the way they could get even with a society that had always treated them as less than equal.

There's no ignoring the fact that Jyoti had her entire life before her—a life that was cruelly, brutally, and remorselessly cut short. She did not deserve to die. She did not deserve to be raped. But somewhere in the entire sequence, we all are equally and collectively responsible for what happened to her. By looking away or blaming her rapists, we cannot shirk the responsibility.

One of the most forceful arguments in favour of the death penalty is that a convict is put in jail at the cost of taxpayers' money: 'Why should we pay for these men who are fed and clothed at our expense?' But is it less expensive to hang a convict? I do not think so. I have handled many criminal cases, and it is only in a death sentence case that I saw such voluminous papers coming to me. The judgments rendered by the lower courts were long, quoting copiously from the law laid down earlier on this subject. Years were spent recording the statements of witnesses.

I am sure all this must have involved a lot of judicial time and money, for capital appeals are not only costly but also time-consuming; litigation costs are more in such cases, including the time of judges and lawyers.

The extra cost of separate death row housing and the need for additional security in the court and elsewhere add to the bill. I am talking of the US, where the number of executions every year is very high. Recently several states in the US, including Nevada, have introduced bills that cite legal costs as one of the reasons for ending the death penalty.[9]

Assuming one should be made to pay for a gruesome murder, what if the accused was framed? Death is irreversible. Suppose, after the execution it is found that the accused was innocent, as is known to happen? Can they ever be brought back to life?

Then why kill them?

Notes

1. 'Death Penalty 2015—Facts and Figures', Amnesty International, 6 April 2016, https://www.amnesty.org/en/latest/news/2016/04/death-penalty-2015-facts-and-figures/, accessed on 22 July 2018.
2. Wikipedia, 'Execution of Clayton Lockett', https://en.wikipedia.org/wiki/Execution_of_Clayton_Lockett, accessed on 22 July 2018.
3. Gomez vs U.S. District Court, 112 5. Ct 1652.
4. Amnesty International USA, 'Death Penalty and Race', nd, https://www.amnestyusa.org/issues/death-penalty/death-penalty-facts/death-penalty-and-race/, accessed on 22 July 2018.
5. Himanshi Dhawan and Pradeep Thakur, 'Here's Proof that Poor Get Gallows, Rich mostly Escape', *Times of India*, 7 August

2015, https://timesofindia.indiatimes.com/india/Heres-proof-that-poor-get-gallows-rich-mostly-escape/articleshow/48151696.cms, accessed on 22 July 2018.

6. Kanimozhi, 'Why the Death Penalty Must End', *Hindu*, 5 June 2017, https://www.thehindu.com/opinion/op-ed/Why-the-death-penalty-must-end/article12057852.ece, accessed on 22 July 2018.

7. Ravji @ Ramchandra vs State of Rajasthan 1996 (2) SCC 175.

8. Surja Ram vs State of Rajasthan Judgment, dated 25 September 1996.

9. Peter A. Collins and Aliza Kaplan, 'The Death Penalty is Getting More and More Expensive. Is It Worth It?', *The Conversation*, 31 March 2017, http://theconversation.com/the-death-penalty-is-getting-more-and-more-expensive-is-it-worth-it-74294, viewed on 28 July.

23

THE DEATH PENALTY CREATES NO DETERRENCE

A bare reading of judgments delivered by Indian courts would show that certain judges have been more inclined to award death penalty than others. My experience has also been the same. Some judges are liberal and eager to study the loopholes in the prosecution's case, while others are stricter. For them, the discrepancies are 'minor' and the prosecution's case remains more or less unaffected.

The empirical study of crime rates in India establishes that the death penalty does not act as a deterrent to crimes of a similar nature. Despite executions of an average of 128 death row convicts per year from 1953 to 1963 as per the 35th report of the Law Commission, the decadal increase in murder cases during the same period as per the National

Crime Records Bureau (NCRB) was about 17 per cent. In fact, there was a drastic reduction in the number of death penalty cases post *Bachan Singh*. As per the NCRB, the decadal decrease in murder cases between 1992 and 2002 was 12.43 per cent despite the growth in India's population by 21.34 per cent. Similarly, the decrease in murder cases between 2002 and 2012 was 1.99 per cent though the population grew from 1.028 billion in 2001 to 1.21 billion in 2011.

Some more hard facts: Statistics prove that the fear of the noose has failed to counter terror offences in the country. Terrorists are fearsome. They don't bat an eyelid while pulling the trigger, regardless of whether they kill innocent men, women, or children. Hang them, make an example of them, and no one else will dare to follow their footsteps. That's what we believe. But is that true? Figures reveal the contrary. The data released by the Ministry of Home Affairs indicates that though no convict from Jammu and Kashmir was executed under the anti-terror laws from 1990 until the execution of Afzal Guru in 2013, Jammu and Kashmir recorded a significant decline in terror incidents, from 5,247 in 1993 to 220 in 2012. The number of persons killed also declined from 2,255 persons in 1993 to 102 in 2012. There was a 70 per cent decrease in terror incidents, and deaths in Jammu and Kashmir fell by 61.66 per cent between 2003 and 2012, as against from 1993 to 2002.

To my mind, there is no point in making an example out of these 'arrows' as Justice Sathasivam called them in the *Mumbai Bomb Blast* case—young, impressionable minds misguided to become terrorists by older masterminds.

What about those who rape and kill? Take the case of Dhananjoy Chatterjee, the guard who, according to the courts, had raped and killed a young girl called Hetal. He was executed in 2004 and people spilled out onto the streets to protest his hanging. Did his execution lead to fewer rapes in the country?

The truth is that the hanging was no deterrence, and incidents of rape did not come down in West Bengal after the event. Again, as per NCRB reports, 1,475 rape cases were reported in West Bengal in 2004. This increased to 1,686 in 2005; 1,731 in 2006; 2,106 in 2007; 2,263 in 2008; 2,336 in 2009; 2,311 in 2010; 2,363 in 2011; and then dropped to 2,046 in 2012. And at the national level, 18,233 rape cases were reported in 2004, which increased to 24,923 in 2012.

I ask the same question: Why hang criminals if it cannot control crime, especially if some of them may actually be innocent or framed? Most heinous crimes are committed in the heat of the moment, when people lose control over their faculties and hardly think of what their action may lead to. By the time they realize what they have done, it is over! Death penalty has hardly been a deterrent in such cases.

Following Jyoti Singh Pandey's gang rape in Delhi on 16 December 2012, the Criminal Law (Amendment) Act, 2013 came into force from 3 December 2014. It introduced the death penalty for repeat offenders of rape under S. 376E of the IPC. Cases of rape have not come down in Delhi even after the amendment.

Now consider the case of the Unites States, where the rate of executions is high. According to Death Penalty Information Center data from 1991 to 2011, states without the death penalty have had consistently lower murder rates when compared to states with the death penalty.

Then why kill the offenders? Give death penalty to none. Because all of them deserve a second chance.

In an article published on 1 August 2015, Shoaib Daniyal[1] talks about the brutalization effect—when there is actually an increase in the murder rate with the death penalty! He says, giving statistics, 'California had higher rates of murder between 1952 and 1967, when it was executing people, as compared to 1968–91 when it wasn't.'

In a study conducted by Bower and Pierce[2] of Northeastern University,[2] it was found that between 1906 and 1963 in New York, murder rates increased on an average in the month following an execution. They found spikes in murder rates following executions. Some police chiefs surveying in the US, too, found the death penalty an area of least concern. 'I have seen the ugliness of murder up close and personal,' said Gregory Ruff, a police officer for 23 years. 'But I have never heard a murder suspect say they thought about the death penalty as a consequence of their actions prior to committing their crimes.'

We have countries like Saudi Arabia, North Korea, Iran, and Somalia, where executions take place in public and in great numbers. The convict is beheaded, stoned, or shot in full public view. All of these measures have failed to reduce the number of crimes. Half of the executions in Saudi Arabia during 2014 were for non-lethal offences including witchcraft, sorcery, and adultery.[3]

China executes its people amid great secrecy, so there is not much data available. No statistics are ever published. Amnesty International stopped publishing estimates for the number of executions in China in 2009 as it was impossible to verify figures while the death penalty remained a state secret.[4] Chinese proverbs like 'killing one to warn a hundred' or 'killing a chicken before a monkey' have all, in some way or the other, talked of the deterrent aspect of the death penalty. The world's leading executioner, China, is believed to kill for offences such as corruption, embezzlement, and drug-related crimes that are not considered capital crimes in other countries. Executions have hardly been a deterrent even in this country.

I have only this to say: when there is nothing to show that hanging, beheading, or roasting a man will help Indian society in any manner whatsoever, then why not discontinue this barbarous practice altogether? After all, two-thirds of the world's countries have already done so.

Notes

1. Shoaib Daniyal, 'Does the Death Penalty act as a Deterrent to Crime?', Scroll, 1 August 2015, https://scroll.in/article/745198/does-the-death-penalty-act-as-a-deterrent-to-crime, accessed on 23 July 2018

2. Evan J. Mandery, *Capital Punishment in America: A Balanced Examination* (Burlington: Jones and Bartlett Learning, 2012).

3. Amnesty International, UK, 'Death Sentence and Executions in 2014: Amnesty International, U.K.', https://www.amnesty.org.uk/world-executions-death-sentences-2014, accessed on 23 July 2018.

4. Amnesty International, UK, 'Death Sentence and Executions in 2014: Amnesty International, U.K.'

24

FOOD FOR THOUGHT

There is no end to the debate: should India abolish the death penalty? Every execution triggers a fresh debate. It was interesting to read different responses to Yakub Memon's hanging in 2015 on social networking sites. He was a dreaded terrorist and many felt he deserved his death. Sparing him would be a great mistake. They felt he should be killed publicly, the way it is done in many Muslim countries. Memon was hanged in Nagpur prison on 30 July 2015 in the early hours. He was declared dead 10 minutes after his execution. It was his 54th birthday. His body was handed over to his brother, Suleiman, and cousin, Usman, on the condition that it would not be displayed publicly. No one wanted further unrest. Memon was finally buried in the Chandanwadi burial grounds at Marine Lines in Mumbai.

I did not want him to be hanged, not because I have a special love for terrorists, but because I felt this killing was not right. Not giving the death penalty does not mean that the culprit gets away; life imprisonment is an equally rigorous punishment. A convict serving life sentence is like an animal in a zoo, without freedom, without liberty. Degraded and forced to wear special jail clothes, they remain within the heavily guarded walls day and night. Theirs is a lonely existence. Visits from family and friends are few.

Most Indian jails are old, overcrowded, and in disrepair. The food served is unfit for consumption. Consider this condition in Seraikala jail in Bihar as reported in the *Economic and Political Weekly* in July 1978:[1] 'The prisoners are invariably very poor, but the food is so rotten they find it revolting...Quite often the prisoners are ordered to lap up the dal which overflows on the floor. For vegetables the prisoners are fed wild grass and roots...A glass of water was found to have no less than one inch of mud at the bottom...For 400 to 800 prisoners, there are just eight latrines. The prisoners, therefore, defecate at the drains. In winter, six of them have to huddle under one blanket...And the prisoners are denied even the "natural habitat" given to animals in zoos....'

Their condition is no better today. I also feel that a system of retributive justice is flawed. It should be restorative: for the victims, the accused, and society. A death sentence is nothing but retribution. It does nothing to restore and certainly does not deter. The death penalty— in fact, any kind of punishment—holds the individual completely responsible for the crime, ignoring the circumstances surrounding the act. Retributive justice is based on the principle of 'an eye for an eye and a tooth for a tooth', with emphasis on the crime being an individual act with individual responsibility. It is nothing but revenge, supporting the argument that people deserve to be treated in the same way they have treated the others.

A system of restoration, on the other hand, sees both the individual and society as equally responsible for a crime. It believes that punishment alone is not effective in changing behaviour. It believes in healing wounds, encouraging offenders to lead law-abiding lives, and repair the harm done to the community.

Most prisoners on death row are not maniacs. They are normal human beings like you and I, with family and friends. I still remember the words of Shyam's brother, as we stood in the corridor, leaning against a pillar right outside the chief justice's court: 'Our mother died last year. She could not take all this anymore.'

I had said nothing in response. What could I say? His brother had been in jail for more than a decade. When both the lower courts had announced a death sentence for Shyam, I did not have much hope. His brother, along with Salim's, would quietly enter the library that I would use to prepare for the case. I would look up and smile. Pointing towards the thick paper books littering the table, I would say, 'Look, I am working on your case.' They were reassured. My heart went out to them. They were young boys, fervently wanting to save their brothers.

But no one from Ramesh's family contacted me—ever. Like a pariah, he was shunned. No one—not the brother, the aunt, or anyone else—ever gave inputs to me as his lawyer. I felt bad. I knew his father was dead and that his mother was differently abled. No one cared for him.

Maybe his mother lay somewhere in a corner in her brother Suryakant's house, thinking of her child who would soon be hanged.

During those times I often thought of my own son—a sweet, naughty little thing who would hide behind a door or under his sister's bed every time I wanted to take him for a wash. And I thought again of Ramesh's mother. But then, we humans are basically shameless. After a while we overcome shock, however great it may be. In a way it is for our own good, for such shocks could make us lose our mental balance.

I wanted my boys to live, though I had never met them.

So once again I return to the same question: why give the death penalty to anyone at all?

Law Commission Recommendations

The Law Commission of India is an executive body. Its major function is to suggest legal reforms and to advise the Ministry of Law and Justice. It consists of experts. I noticed, with a sense of satisfaction, that the 2015 recommendations by the Law Commission were in favour of the abolition of the death penalty, except in cases of terror and war against the state.

The Law Commission Report no. 262 of 2015 titled 'The Death Penalty' discussed in detail the errors and problems in the implementation of the law relating to capital punishment. While considering cases of the non-application of mind, that is, cases in which the authorities did not consider relevant factors that would help them in taking the right decision, it referred to the case of Dhananjoy Chatterjee and observed that when the governor of West Bengal was advised by the government to reject the convict's mercy petition, he was not told about the mitigating circumstances of the case. However, Dhananjoy Chatterjee submitted a mercy petition before the governor again, which was subsequently rejected and he was hanged. The Supreme Court held that to be a serious error that had led to quashing the rejection of the mercy petition.

I have discussed the case of Dhananjoy Chatterjee in my earlier chapter and how lawyers like Colin Gonsalves, who represented him before the top court, hold that his hanging was wrong. A poor man was condemned to death even though all mitigating circumstances were in his favour.

The cases of Ravji Rao and Surja Ram were also considered as examples of wrongful execution and of the failure of the clemency process by the Law Commission. These two cases have also been discussed in detail in earlier chapters: how the two were hanged on the basis of judgments passed by courts that interpreted the law laid down in Bachan Singh's case incorrectly. In Ravji's case[2], the top court had held, 'It is the nature and gravity of crime but *not* the criminal, which are germane for consideration of appropriate punishment in a criminal trial.'

The court, thus, held that the circumstances relating to the making of the criminal were irrelevant and focused only on the circumstances relating to the crime. This was in conflict with the law laid down in Bachan Singh's case. Though Ravji was sentenced to death on the basis of a *per incuriam* judgment (that is, decided without reference to a statutory provision or a previous judgment which would have been relevant), his mercy petition was rejected in just eight days; he was executed on 4 May 1996. Similarly, wrong facts were given in Surja Ram's case and his mercy petition was rejected in 14 days. He was hanged on 7 March 1997. It was a pity that two men were killed because the law was misinterpreted by those hearing their case.

The Report of the Law Commission also made a mention of the 'death row phenomena' that produces physical and psychological conditions of near-torture. This is compounded by the degrading effects of the conditions of incarceration, including solitary confinement.

In its recommendations the Commission suggested measures like police reforms, a witness protection scheme, and a compensation scheme for the victim. It noted the evolution of our jurisprudence—from doing away with the requirement for giving special reasons for imposing life imprisonment instead of death in 1955 to requiring special reasons for imposing capital punishment in 1973; and then a further shift in stand in 1980, when the death penalty was restricted to the rarest of rare cases. This showed the direction in which we were headed.

The Commission then felt that the time had come to move towards the abolition of the death penalty. It was then strongly recommended that capital punishment should be abolished for all crimes other than those relating to terrorism and war, and that the Report would lead to a more rational, principled, and informed debate on the abolition of the death penalty for all crimes.

The time has come for this barbarous system based on retribution and revenge-seeking to be done away with altogether. I do not believe in the system of death by firing squad either, where men in uniform can roast the condemned prisoner. Neither should the criminal be displayed before the public, as is the practice in some Middle-Eastern countries. (In Saudi Arabia they advertise for the post of an executioner, someone who is also supposed to know how to mutilate body parts.) I shudder to think of the executioner whetting the sword and striking the victim's neck, and the bloody head rolling off in full public view.

Changing Laws, and a Senior

Yes, I do not believe in hanging a criminal by the noose, or with a lethal injection, or in the electric chair. But there are many senior lawyers, judges, and legislators who disagree with me. One such person is senior lawyer K.T.S. Tulsi.

Mr Tulsi practises criminal law and was the additional solicitor general of India in 1990. Since 1994, he has been the President of the Criminal Justice Society of India. He has argued many important cases, for instance, the one in which the constitutional validity of TADA was challenged, and also the assassination of former Prime Minister Rajiv Gandhi. He also represented Devinder Pal Singh Bhullar—the 1993 Delhi terror attack convict—and got his death sentence commuted to life imprisonment. In February 2014, Mr Tulsi was appointed a member of the Rajya Sabha.

I got an evening appointment with him. Parking my car under the tall, leafy trees which had langurs swinging from one branch to another, I took quick steps towards his office. A member of Rajya Sabha, Mr Tulsi has been allotted a bungalow in Lutyens' Delhi, where these monkeys are found in abundance. I waited at the reception for some time. It was cold. A young boy, probably his junior, escorted me to his chamber. So what did he have to say on this topic?

Strongly batting for the retention of the death penalty as a form of punishment, Mr Tulsi said, 'India is one of the few countries that has achieved a perfect balance in the use of death penalty in the "rarest of rare cases" and in ensuring that its overuse is avoided.'

He added that its retention has a deterrent effect in cases where no other punishment would suffice. It works best in response to society's need for self-protection and to ensure that future victims are spared. Money is not inexhaustible, especially in a developing country. He felt that the theory of the 'rarest of rare' had worked; the threat of execution accelerated the process of reform.

'But has the death penalty really brought down cases of crime?' I asked. 'Statistics do not say so.' I had done a lot of research on this topic by then, and was ready with my own arguments.

'It is difficult to confirm whether the statistics are correct or not,' he replied. And he had his own reasons. 'The population is rising, and so are cases of crime. Statistics may not reflect the correct situation.'

Mr Tulsi offered his own arguments supporting the retention of the death penalty in the statute books. He feels that execution is a very real punishment where the criminal is made to suffer in proportion with his offence. This deters other criminals. He also believes that capital punishment is used by the state as a means of self-defence. Society does not have the right to risk future victims to spare convicted murderers. Rehabilitation should not be given precedence over deterrence; money is not inexhaustible. The money saved could be utilized by the government for the welfare of the old, the young, and the sick rather than to maintain murderers and rapists. Time and again, in the various decisions rendered by the top court, discussions in parliament and Law Commission reports, it is found that the death penalty is not unconstitutional in light of Article 21 of the Constitution.

However, Mr Tulsi feels that there is a need to restrict its imposition. Care should be taken to ensure that the innocent are not executed, as there is no way of compensating them for miscarriage of justice.

The Indian position on death penalty crystallized in Bachan Singh's case. The problem with the dictum is that there is no reliable pattern under which judges exercise discretion. There have been instances where this irrevocable punishment has been awarded arbitrarily. Moreover, the existing system leads to more death sentences being awarded. The flaw exists both at trial and post-trial stages, and results in death sentences being awarded even when it is unwarranted. The increase in procedures has enhanced death penalty rates—even where substantive law would not have awarded the sentence.

Mr Tulsi suggested that delays—in the disposal of judicial proceedings and in the execution of the death sentence—should be curtailed. The longer a death row convict is kept in prison, the more it costs the government.

He, too, like many others, feels that 'rarest of rare' is highly subjective. He writes that Justice Muralidhar, in his article in 1998,[3] summarized cases where the same crime led to different sentences. Justice Muralidhar is a judge at Delhi High Court who practised law in the Supreme Court before he was elevated to the bench in 2006. Mr Tulsi is of the view that proper guidelines should be formulated to establish the nature of the rarest of rare. One such attempt was made in the form of the Indian Penal Code (Amendment) Bill, 1978, which sought to introduce these guidelines and was passed by the Rajya Sabha. However, the Lok Sabha was dissolved before it could become a law.

The senior lawyer goes on to suggest changing the mode of execution to something more humane. The 187th Report[4] discusses the method of execution by hanging and mutilation. This is contrary to the objectives sought—that it should be speedy and immediately lead to loss of consciousness. Death by a lethal injection is more in consonance with these objectives (the Law Commission is of the same view), being more humane as it brings death within 9 to 14 minutes of being administered.

He concludes by saying that a study of comparative statistics of various countries shows that we have attained a perfect balance regarding awarding the death sentence in the 'rarest of rare' cases. Between 1975 and 1991, 40 persons were executed in India. On an average, two persons have been executed every year. However, the People's Union for Civil Liberties (PUCL) disputes these statistics, Mr Tulsi conceded very fairly. Executions, says PUCL, go unreported. According to them, 1,422 executions took place between 1953 and 1963. This may have included fake encounters and custodial deaths. Even then, he feels, executions have been fewer than in countries like the US and China.

'Money is not inexhaustible,' Mr Tulsi pointed out. But what if by spending this money we are saving an innocent man? Life in prison is better than death. And it isn't true that very few people are getting executed. Many cases of execution go unreported. Who says that if let off, all these convicts will be a threat to society?

report—that the same crime may lead to different
punishments! Is it fair to hang someone when the other
similarly situated person is spared—just because he got a
better lawyer, or the judge who heard his case was more
liberal and believed in the process of reformation?

And just changing the mode of execution will not help.
There have been several cases of botched executions by
lethal injection.

Three Seniors

As a lawyer representing those four unfortunate boys I have
seen things from close quarters. People may call me a rogue
lawyer who fought for those 'devils', as the press called
them soon after the murders on the Nandos hills came to
light. But I have only this to say: every single human life
is sacrosanct. What if those boys were, after all, innocent?
Could I ever forgive myself if they were hanged after the
final hearing in the top court, knowing that their culpability
wasn't proved beyond a shadow of doubt? The officials had
cobbled together some evidence to nail them.

The arguments by my senior, Mr Gonsalves, and me
were long. We pointed out every loophole and flaw in the
prosecution's case. The boys were not beyond reform.
They had, during incarceration, produced a book. They
weren't bloodthirsty hounds who, if let loose, would bleed
society to death. There were all the mitigating factors in
the case—laid down in Bachan Singh's case.

And yet, clamour for the retention of this extreme
penalty is apparent; the legislature has not yet abolished
it despite huge protests after every execution. Why? I

interviewed some senior lawyers who shunned a liberal approach and wanted the death penalty to remain in the statute book.

I spoke to Shekhar Naphade, a reputed senior lawyer from Maharashtra who had fought many high-profile cases in the top court successfully,and sought his views on this subject.

After completing law from Government Law College, Mumbai, Mr Naphade started his law practice in 1974, initially in the Chamber of Mr B.N. Srikrishna who subsequently became a judge of the Supreme Court of India. Mr Naphade was practising mainly on the Original Side of the Bombay High Court. As a part-timer, he taught the Law of Evidence, Administrative Law, and Public International law at the Government Law College from 1976–79. Mr Naphade was designated as Senior Advocate by the Bombay High Court in 1998. He has been appearing in the Supreme Court regularly since 1979.

Mr Naphade has presided over important criminal, civil, and constitutional law matters. One of the important cases relates to the interpretation of S. 154 of the CrPC, popularly known as the *Lalita Kumari* case.[5] Another criminal matter relates to the interpretation of S. 319 of the CrPC. This case is known as *Hardeep Singh vs State of Punjab & Ors. (2014) 3 SCC 92.* He appeared in *Sukanya's* case,[6] which interpreted some of the important provisions of the Arbitration and Reconciliation Act 1996.

Mr Naphade also appeared in a case involving constitutional challenge to the *MCOC Act, Aruna Shanbaug's* case relating to right to live and die with dignity, mercy killing, etc. He has appeared as a Special Counsel for the State of Maharashtra and the State of Tamil

Nadu, among others, and in many important matters in high courts as well as the Supreme Court.

He said, his eyes fixed on the row of books in front of him, as I scribbled on my notepad, 'In the first place, death penalty can be imposed only in the rarest of rare cases. No death should be given if there is possibility of reformation, but if the court is satisfied upon a detailed enquiry (and this is where our system is lacking) that no semblance of humanity is left in the convict, he deserves total extinction. Why should such a convict be left alive and fed at the expense of the state?

'I do not subscribe to the view of eye for an eye and tooth for a tooth. The death penalty is not a method of retribution or organized revenge by the State. This comes from my conviction that imprisonment is meant to facilitate reform. I believe that the organized State is under an obligation to pull out any criminal from the world of crime so that after undergoing the period of incarceration, he or she becomes an asset to society and not a menace.

'Consider this situation: in a war, do you kill all the prisoners? The answer is no. But those who are guilty of brutally killing unarmed civilians would certainly deserve the death sentence. A terrorist who kills innocent human beings deserves death. The organized State should kill such people, as they are a menace to society. The same rule applies to Naxalites, when there is an internal rebellion.'

He concedes that the death penalty should be given only in the rarest of rare cases, but what are those rarest of rare cases? For judge A, the case may call for mercy, but judge B may opine that the under trial deserves nothing

172

less than death. And for many trial court judges in India, every murder case falls in the category of the rarest of the rare.

A terrorist deserves nothing less than death. But is it fair to hang a young man who was just a pawn in the hands of those who have escaped the gallows—just because the latter had money and influence? It is only the henchmen who get caught in such cases; the real brain behind such horrible crimes remains safe.

Mr Naphade paused. I put my pen down. And then he continued, 'I do not believe in the law laid down in the Swamy Shraddananda case.' He tried interpreting the law laid down in that case to me. 'You see,' he said, with some emphasis, 'The law of the land does not contemplate imprisonment for 30–40 years. The minimum sentence under S. 302 is life imprisonment while the maximum is death. Life is construed as biological life. Only the executive can consider remission on the basis of circumstances; in my view keeping a convict in prison for 30–40 years is more inhuman than hanging him. Such prolonged detention will make him more hardened and a greater burden to society.'

If a person is given life imprisonment for committing murder, the government has the power to commute or remit the sentence under Sections 432 and 433 of the CrPC. However, S. 433A, which was introduced in the CrPC by way of an amendment in 1978, provides that the person serving a life sentence cannot be released from prison unless they have been there for at least 14 years. The judges in Swamy Shraddananda's case wanted him to remain in prison throughout his life with no remission. This was wrong interpretation of law, Mr Naphade said, for the courts had no power to give such a direction.

Mr Andhyarujina, another senior whom I interviewed later, seemed to be of the same view. And I made a note of that.

I went to other people and asked them for their views on this issue. I approached Justice V.V.S Rao, a former judge of the Andhra Pradesh High Court, presently practising in the Supreme Court. He is a post graduate in Criminology and Forensic Science. He was the vice president and working president of International Jurists' Organization, Andhra Pradesh Chapter, and also a member of Indo-US Legal Study Team, 1996, constituted by the High Court of Andhra Pradesh. Mr Rao had dealt with many criminal cases as he sat on the bench, coming down with a heavy hand every time a criminal case came up before him.

He looked up, smiled, and asked why I had come to him. As I explained, he began speaking: 'The death penalty has been recognized in all civilized societies—and for a reason. Indian society is not mature enough to do away with this extreme punishment.'

He felt that this has been the view of most judges, barring a few, namely, Justice Sathasivam, who had heard my case. He went on to say that when he read the judgments rendered by the high court and the trial court in Jyoti Pandey's case, he was shocked.

'It was horrific—the brutal manner in which she was killed—and the impact was such that I could not sleep for a few days. We may have advanced greatly economically, but our mindset is still the same. In a few decades, we may become an economic superpower, but there has been no corresponding change socially. The death penalty gives a feeling of justice to the victim and his family. We have a bullock-cart technology society, and people in such a society do not deserve modern principles of reformation in criminal jurisprudence.'

'But Law Commissions have made recommendations for the abolition of the death sentence several times,' I said. 'As late as in 2015, there was a recommendation to scrap this and give death only in terror related cases.'

'The Law Commissions may have recommended the abolition of the death sentence altogether,' he answered, 'but the Legislature has refused to do away with this extreme punishment—and rightly so.'

And then I approached V. Mohana. She is one of the few women lawyers who have been designated a senior by the Supreme Court. When I spoke to her, I found that Ms Mohana did not want to do away with this kind of punishment. But she had her own reasons—and strong ones.

Ms Mohana started her practice as a civil trial lawyer in 1988 in Coimbatore, Tamil Nadu. She shifted to Delhi in 1992 where she had enough exposure both to civil as well as criminal law. After she became an advocate on record in the Supreme Court in 1996 and post empanelment with the Supreme Court Legal Aid Services, a lot of criminal cases came to her. She was designated a senior by the Supreme Court in April 2015.

She said, with a faraway look, 'Though a strong voice has been raised against the death penalty in recent times, barbaric cases are on the rise. There are various theories of punishment: deterrent, retributive, reformative, etc. The Indian Penal Code provided the death penalty for very few offences. However, after the amendment of the Indian Penal Code in 2013, the death penalty is being granted more often in cases of offences against women. Why? This is in response to society's cry for justice.'

She said emphatically that death should be the ultimate punishment imposed in all cases of murder, gang rape, etc. There are gruesome rape and murder cases where death penalty alone can act as a deterrent.

I shook my head, 'But statistics do not say so!'

The senior stuck to her ground. 'If you say that there are statistics to show that the death penalty has not brought down crimes, the same logic applies to other crimes. Should the system of punishment be scrapped altogether?'

She continued, very slowly, as she explained her stand to me, 'Say, for example, the amendment of 2013 in the Indian Penal Code provides for death penalty in case of repeat offenders of rape. Statistics may show that cases of rape have not gone down, but the point is, how many people are aware of this change in law? The actual provisions of law are not even brought to the notice of the common man. Unless such awareness is created, the common man will not be in a position to understand the consequences of any action or omission on his part.

'Despite a growing demand for the abolition of the death penalty, the reason our legislature has not only retained it but also brought new and graver offences within its ambit shows popular will. Newer and graver offences are on rise—acid attacks, rapes, and murders. Some of the offenders are repeat offenders. There will be no deterrence if the death penalty is not retained. Human rights are not only for the accused but also for the victims. A wrong signal will be sent if the violators are not punished.'

To protect innocent people from getting falsely implicated, Ms Mohana suggested certain remedial measures: 'The sessions judge who conducts trial needs adequate training before she or he can judge a case where the offence is punishable with death. So if training is given at that stage, there will be fewer chances of cases being wrongly decided. The judges will also know what factors carry weight while imposing punishment.'

Talking about Sriharan's case (he was the prime culprit in Rajiv Gandhi's assassination) in which she had argued for the State, she said that one of the arguments advanced by the defence was that languishing in jail for more than 20 years was worse than the death sentence for the culprits.

'Why can't this situation be remedied by reducing administrative delays as well as delays in courts?' she added. 'When you look at statistics, you will find very few of those convicted have been hanged. Though a large number of capital punishments are handed down at the trial court stage, they are generally commuted to something less severe by the high court or the Supreme Court.'

'What about the mental agony of the person on death row? They are kept in solitary confinement, and the sword of Damocles hangs over their head till their case is finally decided by the top court. There have been instances of convicts losing their minds, for instance, Devinder Pal Singh Bhuller,the Sikh terrorist on death row for the1993 terror attack. What do you have to say to this?' I asked.

'You need to see the mental agony and human rights of the victim and his family too,' my senior responded calmly. 'Take the case of Ajmal Kasab [the Pakistani terrorist who attacked Mumbai in 2008]. Look at the kind of terror he unleashed and the number of people he killed. Courts are very cautious when it comes to circumstantial evidence. Unless there is direct and incontrovertible evidence, we need not enforce it, unless absolutely necessary. We have the latest judgment of the Supreme Court, which holds that review petitions challenging the death penalty should be heard in open court by three judges.'

This indeed happened in Mohd. Arif's case decided on 2 September 2014, when a bench headed by Chief Justice R.M. Lodha gave a decision providing for open court hearing in cases of review of death penalty by a 4:1 majority. The judgment was written by Justice Rohinton Nariman on behalf of the majority. Justice Chelameshwar had dissented.

'Besides constitutional checks and balances,' the senior continued, 'guidelines are issued by the Supreme Court from time to time. And once the penalty is finally given, after exhausting all the avenues, execution should take place within a reasonable time limit to prevent further mental agony.'

Yes. These lawyers had a point, no doubt. A question that they repeatedly asked was: 'What about the victims? What about their human rights?' They are correct, no doubt. But cops don't always catch the right person and not all witnesses are honest. Sometimes, witnesses are known to have testified against an accused facing a death sentence out of spite or revenge. No one is questioning the criminal justice system. I only have a quarrel with this barbarous, inhuman practice.

And I found, to my great relief, that I was not the only person who thought so. Many other lawyers like me batted for the end of this practice. I set out to interview them and seek their views on the subject.

Some Other Legal Luminaries

I contacted a few senior lawyers with vast experience— much more than mine—who have been closely associated with the evolution of death penalty laws in India. They have fought for clients similar to the ones I represented. How was their experience? Did they feel the way I felt? What were their views? I wanted to know.

Justice Mukul Mudgal is the former Chief Justice of Punjab and Haryana High Court who, as a lawyer, practised at the Delhi High Court and the Supreme Court, before he was elevated as a judge in the Delhi High Court in 1998. He was closely associated with *Bachan Singh*, the landmark judgment that became the touchstone for the sentencing policy regarding every murder case in our country. If there was one case that changed the attitude of the courts towards those who killed, it was this.

Though the death penalty was not abolished altogether, the approach of the judiciary became more humane, much more than it had been earlier. When I met Justice Mudgal, he tried to remember events of three-and-a-half decades ago —about how the doctrine of the 'rarest of the rare' had evolved.

'The case was argued by Dr Y.S. Chitale, my senior. I was his advocate on record,' he said. 'During the course of the hearing, four judges were against the striking down of capital punishment and only Justice Bhagwati was in its favour. Dr Chitale asked me to go through all the Supreme Court judgments where death had been reduced to life and prepare a short summary of the reasoning in all such cases. Since we thought we were not making any progress in challenging capital punishment, these arguments were put in the form of written submissions, giving rise to the doctrine of "rarest of the rare", which is nothing but a summary of Supreme Court judgments reducing death to life.'

After we lawyers have made our arguments verbally in the courtroom, we file our submissions in writing in order to supplement the arguments. This way all the points missed or overlooked in the courtroom are taken care of. Bachan Singh's lawyers had known they were losing, so they had made one last attempt to get some relief from the court. Based on their written note, the judges laid down the law that the death penalty should be awarded only in the rarest of cases.

'But why has the death penalty not been abolished in India even now—35 years after *Bachan Singh*? After all, many countries in the world have taken that step,' I asked. Having been on both sides—the bar and the bench—I felt Justice Mudgal would be the best person to throw some light on this aspect.

'It is for the legislature to do so if it feels there is a need,' was his crisp reply. 'The judiciary can also do it, just as was the minority view in case of *Bachan Singh*.'

This is exactly what Justice Anaga Kumar Patnaik had told me years ago, when I went to meet him after an appointment. He retired as a judge of the Supreme Court in 2014 and was known for his contagious smile as he conducted court proceedings. I had appeared before him on a few occasions. He was a pro-poor judge who supported the underprivileged. Justice Patnaik was made the chairman of the Supreme Court Legal Aid Services Committee by the then chief justice, Justice Sarosh Homi Kapadia.

'If you feel so strongly about the death penalty, you should challenge *Bachan Singh*,' he had told me. 'It is for the legislature to abolish it.'

'But Justice Satya Brata Sinha did say that the death penalty should go, even though Justice Markandey Katju's response was, "Who are we to do it? It is for the legislature to do so," I interjected. Of course, I was referring to Swamy Shraddananda. Justice Patnaik smiled broadly and looked at me the way one looks at a child who has asked a big question.

I spoke to many lawyers, mostly senior people in my profession. As I have mentioned earlier, Colin Gonsalves is well known for his strong views on human rights and has had made a substantial contribution in this field. He had also been my guide and mentor in the Nandos hills case. I decided to ask him a few questions as well.

'When so many other countries have abolished the death penalty, why have we not done so, especially in the land of Gandhi?'

He replied without hesitation, 'We have still not abolished the death penalty in the land of Gandhi since we are probably one of the most violent countries in the world. Violence has got into the psyche of the rulers. It is a myth that India is non-violent. The notions of revenge and retribution are the dominant attitude as far as the ruling classes are concerned.'

'Will hanging one or two people really bring about deterrence?'

'Not at all. On the contrary, when you hang people you spur greater levels of violence and crime. Brutality by the State has a rippling and magnified effect on civil society. The State has to be calm and dignified in the face of provocation and aggression. It must be non-violent even if its people are the opposite. In India, the State is the biggest terrorist because it uses torture and cruelty against the poor all the time.'

'Any particular case you can remember?' I asked.

'Yes. The case of Om Prakash. He was a juvenile said to have murdered a family. None of the three courts—the trial court, the high court and the Supreme Court—while exercising their jurisdiction under Article 136 of the Constitution, saw the boy's school-leaving certificate. In the last case, an Article 32 petition was filed, yet again, saying that the school-leaving certificate had not been shown. The court, to its credit, held that the certificate proving that he was a juvenile had not been considered and released him. The boy is now happily married and has his own children.'

When we speak of juveniles, we take their immature mind into consideration. Children are unaware of the consequences of their acts. This is why the laws show mercy to a juvenile delinquent. Suppose my 12-year-old son picked up a kitchen knife, something which is easily available in every household, and suddenly stabbed someone while playing. Would he deserve a death sentence? The laws say no. The criminal justice system is based upon intention and knowledge. Even though it may seem otherwise, the truth is that most juveniles—even when they kill someone—don't really realize the full impact or consequence of their actions. They have not seen much of life; their experience is very limited. When did they have the occasion to learn such major life lessons? Where was the opportunity for spiritual growth? Most of them never intended to take away a life. They are not like adults who, knowing everything well enough, made a conscious decision to choose evil.'

'What would you say about the hanging of Dhananjoy Chatterjee, whom you represented as a lawyer?' I asked next.

This was an important case. Dhananjoy had been a simple watchman from a poor family. 'If you have a panel of retired judges of the Supreme Court looking at the evidence in Dhananjoy Chatterjee's case today, I have no doubt he will be found innocent,' said Mr Gonsalves. 'The time has come for the judiciary to declare the death penalty as unconstitutional. And *Swamy Shraddananda*, in which the judges held that the convict should remain in prison throughout his life, was only a half-way solution. Though it is unfair, excessive, and disproportionate, at least it is better than death.'

Murderers—if indeed they are murderers—never get away after committing the crime. They are beaten up by cops, rot in jail in unhygienic conditions, and lead a life that is far from normal. Finally, when—if at all—they are set free after 14 or 20 years in prison, they have already lost most of their life. They have suffered enough. Keeping them in prison for theis entire life is not the solution, if the aim of the justice system is to reform and rehabilitate a criminal— which is the ideal it should aim towards. The theory of retribution is not approved of by many in the world.

'And has the "rarest of the rare" formula worked? Isn't it subjective?' I continued.

'Yes, it is subjective. Chief Justice Dattu reversed Chief Justice Sathasivam's approach, and gave some deplorable judgments,' said Mr Gonsalves. Chief Justice Sathasivam went on to convert many death penalty cases to life imprisonment, as he had done in my case. However, Chief Justice Dattu, then the outgoing chief justice, confirmed many death penalties.

Maybe I can understand Chief Justice Dattu's thoughts and decisions. Judges hardly speak their mind. We get a rare insight on a few occasions when they speak at public functions. I remember attending the farewell party of an outgoing judge in which he gave a farewell speech and described her as Goddess Durga, who vanquished demons! Perhaps he truly viewed criminals as demons who needed to be removed from the face of the Earth. But then, as Mr Gonsalves said, hanging anyone is hardly a solution. The real issue that needs to be addressed is much larger.

Now I had another question. 'What about the socio-economic and religious backgrounds of those who have been hanged? Don't they count?'

'If you are poor and belong to a minority class, your chances of getting the death sentence are ten times more than if you are economically comfortable and part of the majority. The criminal judiciary is institutionally communal and Muslims in the criminal justice system, in particular, start with the disadvantage of being presumed guilty.'

Was the senior lawyer referring to the hanging of Ajmal Kasab and Yakub Memon, the two Muslim terrorists who were part of two separate conspiracies that led to the deadliest attacks on Mumbai? An example had to be made out of them and, therefore, they were hanged.

Ajmal Kasab was a Pakistani militant and a member of Lashkar-e-Taiba. He was caught after the terror attacks in Mumbai in 2008. Apparently, a sinister conspiracy had been hatched in Pakistan, leading to a savage attack on Mumbai by a team of 10 terrorists, including Kasab, who reached the city through the Arabian Sea.

Born on 13 September 1987, Kasab lived in Faridkot in Pakistan. His father worked on carts for a living. Later, Kasab joined the jihadi forces, constantly convinced by

Amir Hafeez Sayeed that all Mujahideens must fight for the independence of Kashmir.

Kasab and his accomplices used to practise with Kalashnikovs (AK-47s). Armed with these guns, and hand grenades, they landed on the shores of Mumbai. Kasab acted like a butcher. He decapitated the man who had acted as the navigator in the boat that had brought him to India.

The attack in Mumbai began on 26 November 2008 at about 9.15 p.m. and ended when the last of the attackers—holed up in Hotel Taj Mahal Palace—was killed by Indian security forces on 28 November. The terrorists killed 166 people and injured 238; property worth Rs 150 crore was lost. The image of the young Pakistani with a haversack on his back and an AK-47 in his hands was etched in the minds of Indians for a long time.

'Would you like to say something about Yakub Memon and Kasab?' I asked Mr Gonsalves. Memon had been hanged on his birthday. The Supreme Court had heard the final plea from his lawyers late into the previous night. Still, the judges refused to spare him. The bigger fish sitting in Pakistan are, even at this moment, enjoying luxurious lives, while our country decided to make an example out of this man.

'All hanging is wrong, but I always feel that a person like Kasab who had been sold to the Taliban at the age of 13 and indoctrinated, could have been reformed,' my senior responded thoughtfully.

'If the terrorists are let off, there could be a repeat of Kandahar, isn't it? Isn't that what some people are afraid of? But do you think terrorists—the brainwashed jihadis—are completely beyond reform?'

'Whether to bargain with terrorists or not is for the State to decide,' Mr Gonsalves sighed. 'If some terrorist says that A, B, or C should be released, the State should not accept it.' He paused. 'If the terrorists have been brainwashed, in a proper rehabilitation set-up they can be brainwashed yet again to become good human beings. It depends on how you treat them.'

I now wanted to talk to the lawyers of Kasab and Memon. What did they think about the terrorists they had defended?

The Supreme Court had agreed to hear two petitions challenging the death warrant issued against Yakub Memon. While one was filed on behalf of Yakub Memon, the other intervening application was filed by the Centre on the Death Penalty at National Law University, Delhi. Senior advocate Raju Ramachandran appeared for Memon, while T.R. Andhyarujina represented the Centre on the Death Penalty.

Raju Ramachandran, a former additional solicitor general of India, is an alumnus of St Stephen's College, Delhi University, where he studied Economics. He was also appointed as amicus curiae in the case of Ajmal Kasab by the top court. His primary argument was that Kasab did not get a fair trial—an integral part of 'right to life and personal liberty' under Article 21 of the Constitution. He was not apprised of the fact that he was not bound to make a confession. Free legal aid, he had argued further, was an essential ingredient in due process and implicit in the right guaranteed under Article 21. The accused did not get proper legal representation in the beginning at all.

Justice Aftab Alam and Justice Chandramauli Prasad heard the case. I remembered going to the courtroom once or twice when the case was being argued. On the question of sentencing, Mr Ramachandran said that Kasab was barely 21 at the time the offence had been committed, he loved watching Indian movies, and that he had dropped out of school in Standard IV. He used to earn through manual labour before he was co-opted into a group of fidayeens and completely brainwashed by the Lashkar-e-Taiba. He felt that death should be reserved for his handlers, who had managed to escape.

The judgment in the case of Kasab was written by Justice Aftab Alam. The court felt that since the boy never showed any remorse, there was no possibility of his reformation. The only mitigating factor was his young age, which was completely written off by the absence of regret on his part.

Kasab was hanged on 21 November 2012, at the Yerwada Central Jail in Pune. He was 25 when he died.

Unfortunately, the boy displayed no regrets about whatever he had done; he wanted others to follow him and become a fidayeen like him. He was disowned by his own country. Though he had wanted a Pakistani lawyer, no one came to represent him from across the border. He was a misguided youth, a hero in his own eyes.

Mr Ramachandran also represented Yakub Memon at one stage. Memon was the terrorist alleged to be one of the masterminds of the 1993 Mumbai bomb blasts. He was ultimately hanged on 30 July 2015.

Known for his honest approach in the courtroom, Mr Ramachandran is cool and composed when he argues. He told me how he got to argue Kasab's case as we sat in his office, the interior gloom contrasting with the lovely view of the foliage outside.

'When Kasab filed his appeal in the Supreme Court through the jail,' he said, 'apparently the registrar general of the Supreme Court was approached by some lawyers to be appointed as the amicus curiae. The registrar went to the then chief justice, Late Chief Justice Sarosh Homi Kapadia, for instructions. It seems Chief Justice Kapadia told the registrar that he would assign the case to a presiding judge who could then decide how he wanted to go about it. He assigned the case to Justice Aftab Alam who requested me to be the amicus curiae and put forward this case.

'Though I had immediately made up my mind to accept it, I sought a couple of days' time to take my family into confidence, keeping in mind the nature of the case. It was the call of duty. Arguing the case with the assistance of my co-amicus Gaurav Agarwal, Advocate on Record, was a memorable experience. The bench was patient and courteous, and I had the advantage of standing against a fair opponent, my old friend, Gopal Subramanium. I did not face any kind of pressure or threat, and never felt the need to ask for personal security, though many well-meaning friends suggested I should.

'My counterparts in the lower courts must have faced more difficulties as they were in Mumbai, the scene of the dastardly incident. Though we argued the case on its merits, it was an open-and-shut case for the prosecution. I thought there was scope for a powerful argument on the sentence, considering Kasab's young age, his background of economic deprivation, his being brainwashed by extremist ideologies at a young and impressionable age, and the fact that he was but a pawn in the hands of larger forces who remained out of the reach of law. I did my best to convince the court, though I failed. As I said then,

I bow down to the verdict of the court and I will say nothing more.'

Kasab had, no doubt, done something deplorable. And I repeat: I don't have a soft corner for terrorists who kill and maim innocent people. But then, why make an example of a young boy who was brainwashed while the real culprits are still alive, trying to poison others?

And then I approached Tehmtan R.Andhyarujina, another stalwart in the profession. I wanted to hear his views too on this volatile subject. He was the solicitor general of India from 1996 to 1998. Though selected for Indian Foreign Services in 1958, he had chosen to practise law. He had opposed Yakub Memon's hanging and argued against it in the Supreme Court, before the convict was finally hanged.

'Do you believe in the death penalty?' I asked him when we got to meet and I began to discuss the subject tentatively with him.

'I do not believe in the death penalty.' His voice was firm, which was encouraging.

'Why do you think the death penalty should be done away with?' I pressed on.

'The formula of "rarest of the rare" does not work; it is highly subjective. Whether it acts as a deterrent or not is anybody's guess. Statistically, it has been proved in all countries that it does not operate as a deterrent. The family of the victim may want to hang the accused, but the State should not be influenced. The larger interest of society should be considered.

'Hanging is often botched. Even in the US where they give lethal injection instead, there have been some horror stories. All of them are a glaring example of how a man is subjected to great agony. In India especially, the disposal of petitions and pleas takes a lot of time. A mercy petition takes at least four or five years before it is finally decided. It is a matter of politics whether a particular person on death row should be hanged or not. Take, for instance, the case of Afzal Guru. His mercy plea was secretly dismissed on the eve of election and he was hanged in Tihar jail. In the US too, the sentencing is a prolonged affair and there have been many cases of miscarriages.'

'You argued against Yakub Memon's hanging, which set off a fresh debate on whether the death penalty should be given at all. Would you like to speak about it?'

'Yakub, a conspirator in the Mumbai bomb blast, went away to Pakistan. It was later on disclosed by RAW officers that he had come to the country on an assurance that he would not be hanged. The prosecution chose to not mention it during the arguments. However, this fact came to light on the eve of his execution. The second mercy plea had grounds missing in the first: that he had come to India on an assurance! The Home ministry persuaded the president to dismiss it. The Supreme Court refused to interfere. Yakub Memon was ultimately hanged at 6 in the morning.'

Mr Andhyarujina was also of the view that the judiciary does not have the power of remission. For instance, in the Swamy Shraddananda case, Justice Aftab Alam held that the swamy had to remain in prison throughout his life. The former solicitor general questioned the law laid down in *Swamy Shraddananda*. 'Convictions and remissions are two different aspects. The power of remission is in the hands of the executive—no judgment can say that a convict can have no remission, for this is contrary to the provisions of CrPC and even the Constitution.'

He was against the court holding that a convict should remain in prison throughout his life; the judiciary simply did not have such powers.

So the debate is on. While some, including Justice Katju and Justice Patnaik, may feel that if at all the death penalty has to be abolished in India, it is for the legislature to do so. The job of the court, they feel, is to interpret laws, not make them. The Constitution provides for a separation of powers. The power of making laws rests with the legislature. Many senior lawyers, on the other hand, including Mr Gonsalves and Mr Andhyarujina, want the death penalty to go—whether it is done by the legislature or by a judicial order. And I totally agree with them. This primitive practice of hanging people must simply be done away with.

Notes

1. Arun Sinha, 'The Horrors of Seraikela Jail', *Economic and Political Weekly*, 22 July 1978, Volume 13, Issue No 2.9.
2. Ravji @ Ramchandra vs State of Rajasthan 1996 (2) SCC 175
3. Dr. S. Muralidhar, 'Hang Them Now, Hang Them Not : India's Travails With The Death Penalty', Journal of Indian Law Institute (1998), P. 143
4. Law Commission of India, '187th report of Law Commission on Mode of Execution of Death Sentence & Incidental Matters', October 2003.
5. Lalita Kumari vs Govt. of U.P. and Ors. (2014) 2 SCC 1
6. Sukanya Holdings Pvt. Ltd. vs Jayesh H. Pandya & Anr. Date of judgment: 14 April 2003